ECONOMICS
Data Response
Questions Answered

J Harris
MA, BSC(ECON)

E S Janes
BSC(ECON)

Pitman

PITMAN PUBLISHING LIMITED
128 Long Acre, London WC2E 9AN

PITMAN PUBLISHING INC
1020 Plain Street, Marshfield, Massachusetts 02050

Associated Companies
Pitman Publishing Pty Ltd, Melbourne
Pitman Publishing New Zealand Ltd, Wellington
Copp Clark Pitman, Toronto

© J Harris and E S Janes

First published in Great Britain 1985

British Library Cataloguing in Publication Data

Harris, J.
  Economics data response questions answered.
  1. Economics—Problems, exercises, etc.
  I. Title   II. Janes, E.S.
  330'.076   HB171.5

ISBN 0-273-02174-5

Typeset in 10/11 pt Linotron 202 Bembo and printed in
Great Britain at The Pitman Press, Bath

Contents

Preface

The Data Response type of question paper has become increasingly important as a means of examining Economics, particularly at A level. Several GCE boards use this method and the London board has done so to a significant extent since 1977. Many candidates feel doubtful about what is required of them and the purpose of this book is to show how questions of this nature can be approached, and to provide examples of possible answers to selected past questions. In order to give as wide a coverage of the core syllabus as possible the authors have included a selection of questions which they have devised themselves, and to which answers are suggested.

The University of London University Entrance and School Examinations Council accepts no responsibility whatsoever for the accuracy or method of working in the answers given.

An identical disclaimer is also made by the following:

The Associated Examining Board
The Southern Universities Joint Board

The authors wish to express their thanks to these boards for permission to make use of their questions, the answers suggested being entirely the responsibility of the authors. It is hoped that users of this book will not only find it useful in improving their skills in dealing with Data Response questions, but will also find it helpful in revision for A level, first degree courses and some professional examinations in Economics.

1

Data Response Techniques

1 GENERAL

Success in answering these questions depends upon a methodical approach by the candidate. The first essential is to read the entire question with care in order to recognise as far as possible the area of knowledge which is being tested and which specific principles from this area are inherent in the material presented by the question. In many question papers the candidate is allowed an element of choice. Where this is the case *all* questions should be read through once before a final choice is made of those to be attempted. Having made this choice it is best to start by answering first the question which seems to be the easiest. At this point it is important to make a quick calculation of the amount of time that can be spent on each answer in relation to the marks which the questions carry. As an example, if the total marks for a question amount to 20 and there is a maximum of 60 marks for a 2 hour paper, then no longer than 35–40 minutes should be spent on that question. Examiners have a right to expect that Economics candidates are familiar with the concept of equi-marginal returns and that they will apply that principle. A short time should be left at the end of the examination so that what has been written can be checked critically before handing in the answers.

In answering the questions it should be noted that a great many questions have been carefully structured by the examiner (i.e. there are clearly distinguished parts of the question). Candidates should use the same structuring for their answers and, where marks for each part of the question are given, each part of the question should be allocated the appropriate amount of time. Questions which are structured usually have parts which reflect increasing difficulty, so it is important to be sure that an attempt can be made at *all* parts of the question.

Many questions require the calculation and/or manipulation of figures. Whilst most examining boards allow the use of electronic calculators, candidates save time if they are able quickly to make

1

rough calculations mentally of percentages, ratios, fractions and decimals. This approach is of particular use in dealing with questions based on elasticities of demand and/or supply and with questions about profit margins and cost changes. However, accurate arithmetic is often required and answers given to earlier parts of a question may have to be used as input to a later part of that question. Hence the need for accurate working. These questions which require calculations often require the calculations to be related to specific laws or principles, e.g. the law of diminishing returns; candidates should be able to state, as well as apply, that law or principle and define economic terms as required.

Where questions give statistics for manipulation and/or comment the candidate should see if the data is hypothetical or has been collected from real life. In making comment on the former, most points of valid economic theory may well be accepted in the answer. It is also necessary to illustrate points with actual examples where relevant. In the latter case the candidate should try to relate knowledge of recent past economic events to the data provided, thus showing that essential awareness of the link between theory and the real world. Whenever numerical examples are involved candidates should show a sense of realism in the degree of accuracy in the arithmetic required. There is, for example, no sense in working even to the nearest £10,000 when answering questions about national income.

Other questions do not involve facility in numeracy so much as the ability to comprehend and comment upon pieces of prose taken from books, newspapers or magazines. Answers to these questions demand knowledge of current economic events and how these illustrate the application of the laws and principles of the subject. Candidates need to be particularly precise in their use of English and spelling so that their meaning is clearly conveyed to the examiner. It is also important on reading the question to pick out the truly relevant from the less relevant information. Underlining the truly relevant parts of the question may help in the quick reference back to the question as the answer is developed.

Candidates must always be on their guard against irrelevancy in their answers. The real damage is done to the chances of the candidate by the fact that irrelevant answers earn no marks but, at the same time, valuable time has been wasted which could have been used to gain marks on another question.

In the experience of the authors a common cause of the failure of candidates to do themselves justice is a lack of planning of answers. A plan is essential to the logical development of any answer and a plan, even if only consisting of paragraph headings, should appear at the start of each answer. The plan should be ruled through neatly once when it has been used. This indicates that it is not a part of the final answer. If time is pressing, jot down your thoughts about the points you wish to make and then number them for inclusion in your final answer.

2 ECONOMIC NUMERACY

Numerical data can be displayed in a wide variety of forms such as graphs, tables, charts and diagrams. The objective is to present information which will test the candidate's economic numeracy through questions which demand comprehension, analysis and application of economic principles to data not previously seen.

With numerical questions it is important to understand the differences between time-series and cross-sectional data, percentages and index numbers, constant prices and current prices, seasonally adjusted and seasonally unadjusted figures. Some questions ask students to distinguish between different formats and to explain the advantages and limitations of each. On the other hand, candidates should not merely repeat statistical data in sentence form when this has not been asked for.

Numerical and statistical data will often convey more information than a prose passage of the same length. It is important to understand the material thoroughly, and care should be taken in examining time spans, denominations, rates of change, scales and footnotes. Economic numeracy requires skills of selection. While students should be aware of all the facets relating to the data, the candidate must choose those elements which pertain to each part of a question. It is not necessary to refer to every single item in a large mass of data simply because it has been made available. In other words, relevancy is essential.

Data will sometimes obscure as much as it reveals and it is perfectly valid for a candidate to make reference to the inadequacy of statistics where appropriate. This may involve, for example, noting any omissions, calculating percentage changes where data is expressed in absolute terms, and questioning the relevance of statistical averages. Although students are expected to be proficient in analysing the data supplied, additional relevant material can be included in answers. Recent economic events can be used to support or contest conclusions drawn from the data provided, especially if the candidate considers it to be incomplete.

Where calculations are required, working should be shown and explained so that the candidate is not penalised for lack of economic knowledge when, in fact, an arithmetic error has been made. Finally, the answer should show evidence of being planned logically.

3   ECONOMIC LITERACY

These questions present candidates with an extract from a book, newspaper, journal or other periodical and invite comment on, or explanation of, points contained in the extract. Candidates may also be required to make projections from the information given; so it is important to note carefully the source and date of the information and see whether that source is likely to take an objective or a subjective view. If the latter is the case the candidate does not necessarily have to agree with the view expressed if a logical argument can be put up in favour of a different view. A good answer should begin with concise definitions of the key economic terms or concepts employed in the question. One should then show awareness of any value judgements or unsupported statements contained in the extract being discussed; it would be rash to rely on these in coming to a conclusion.

Facts given in the question also need careful attention since it is often possible to interpret these in different ways, and the examiner may be looking for evidence in your answer that you have not taken one isolated view of the facts. Questions often provide an opportunity to refer to current events and candidates can prepare themselves by regular critical reading of reliable newspapers, bank reviews and Treasury *Economic Progress Reports*. Any significant item of economic news is a possible source of a future question, and such items which have appeared at a later date than that on which the question item was written may afford the means of making comparisons and contrasts with the original extract.

Answers should follow a logically developed plan, but candidates need to eliminate political bias from their work and avoid taking a dogmatic attitude. The examiner is looking for sound economic argument and the realisation that economic problems usually have more than one solution.

2

Answers with Explanatory Notes

QUESTION 1—MAXIMISING PROFITS/MINIMISING LOSSES

Given below are the cost and price data for a profit maximising firm.

Output level (per period)	Total variable costs (£)	Total fixed costs (£)
1	5	5
2	9	5
3	12	5
4	16	5
5	22	5
6	31	5
7	34	5
8	52	5
9	76	5
10	107	5

(a) Assume that the market price is constant at £18 per unit. At what level of output would profits be maximised?
(b) If the market price were to decline from £18, at what prices would the firm cease production (i) in the long run and (ii) immediately?
(c) If total fixed costs were to double to £10, explain the effects on your answers to parts (a) and (b).

[June 1981, London]

NOTES ON ANSWERING THE QUESTION

The question gives figures relating to a firm's cost structure and tests the candidate's knowledge of the theory of the firm.

Part (a) requires the profit maximising output. This can be calculated by using either total cost/revenue curves or marginal cost/revenue curves. Both methods are acceptable.

5

Part (*b*) requires calculation of the average total costs (ATC) and the average variable costs (AVC) at each level of output. The break-even price occurs at the lowest point on the ATC curve since the firm will make a loss if the price falls below this level (£5.25). However, if the price does fall below £5.25, the firm may be able to minimise its losses by continuing production in the short run. So long as the price covers the AVC the loss is less than the fixed costs which would be incurred if the output is zero. If the price falls below the minimum point of the AVC curve (£4.00) the firm will shut down, even in the short run.

In other words, the long-run supply curve of an individual firm is that part of its marginal cost (MC) curve which lies above its ATC curve. Its short-run supply curve is that part of its MC curve which lies above its AVC curve.

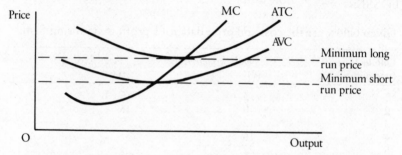

Part (*c*) uses the same principles. Since MC and AVC are not affected, answers to part (*a*) and (*b*)(ii) do not alter. However, the extent to which ATC changes as a result of the change in fixed costs must be calculated to find the lowest point on the new ATC curve.

SUGGESTED ANSWER

Calculations

Output	Marginal cost	AVC	ATC (F.C. = £5)	ATC (F.C. = £10)
	(£)	(£)	(£)	(£)
1	5	5.0	10.0	15.0
2	4	4.5	7.00	9.5
3	3	4.0	5.66	7.33
4	4	4.0	5.25	6.5
5	6	4.4	5.4	6.4
6	9	5.166	6.00	6.83
7	3	4.857	5.57	6.28
8	18	6.5	7.125	7.75
9	24	8.44	9.00	9.55
10	31	10.7	11.2	11.7

(*a*) Profits are maximised at the level of output where marginal cost is equal to marginal revenue. Marginal revenue remains constant at £18, indicating a perfectly competitive market. Marginal cost is equal to £18 at output 8. The producer would merely break even on the 8th unit and can, therefore, maximise profits at either output 7 or 8.

(*b*)(i) The firm will cease production in the long run if average revenue fails to cover average total cost. If the price declines to a level below that represented by the lowest point on the ATC curve, there is no level of output at which the firm could make a profit, and the firm would cease production. This occurs at a price of £5.25.

(ii) A firm will continue to operate at a loss, in the short run, provided that its revenue is greater than its variable costs. Fixed costs are incurred even if the output is nil. The difference, therefore, between revenue and variable costs will help to cover these unavoidable expenses. Consequently the firm will cease production in the short run if there is no level of output at which average revenue can cover average variable costs. This situation arises when the price falls below the lowest point on the AVC, i.e. at £4.00.

(*c*) Since a change in fixed costs does not affect marginal costs, the profit maximising output remains the same, although profits will be reduced by £5.00. Doubling fixed costs would, however, affect average total cost. Again the firm would continue to produce in the long run so long as price exceeded the lowest point on the ATC curve, but this will now rise to £6.28. Like marginal costs, average variable costs are not affected by a change in fixed costs and the firm would still continue to produce in the short run so long as price does not fall below £4.00.

QUESTION 2—COMPETITION IN THE AIRLINE INDUSTRY

'Pan Am has formerly been the unchallenged leader of the airline industry. Last week it announced price cuts on an unprecedented scale. Is that the long-awaited death-rattle or the first sign of a new aggressive Pan Am?

Pan Am is axing its fares on all transatlantic routes by up to 60%. These cuts take their prices right down into Laker's own cut price preserve. (Laker had pioneered low price transatlantic air travel.) There is scarcely an airline left unharmed. British Airways and TWA are reluctantly following suit; British Caledonian face new, cheaper competition on the economy fare to Houston. Sir Freddie Laker has complained to the Department of Trade about Pan Am's "predatory" attack.

Pan Am's move reverses the industry's drive to get fares up and goes against what British Airways thought was a consensus. Hope of boosting fare yields as part of the latter's salvation plan now look slim—the industry is locked into the cycle of price cut feeding on price cut.

The North Atlantic has always been a heartbreaking route for airlines; in and out of the red but too important to ignore. The total cost to the average airline of operating a wide-bodied 747 between London and New York is between $75,000 and $90,000 for the one-way trip. Breakeven occurs with about half the 402 seats filled on a 747. In the depth of winter this is difficult to achieve and traffic is down this year.

What has stung Laker most is that they were about to launch a Regency Class, replacing 82 economy seats with 46 generously sized and spaced armchairs. With free champagne and menus this was aimed at businessmen, just about the only substantial winter market on the North Atlantic.'   (Source: *The Sunday Times*)

With reference to costs, capacity and competition, what economic rationale can you offer for the situation described in the above passage?
[*June 1983, London*]

NOTES ON ANSWERING THE QUESTION

This question concentrates on micro-economic analysis of market behaviour. Therefore, the type of market situation needs to be identified and the following phrases in the question help to do this: 'leader of the airline industry', 'Laker's own cut price preserve', 'price cut feeding on price cut', and 'aimed at businessmen'.

These phrases point to the existence of oligopolistic competition in which there is:

(*a*) an established price maker,
(*b*) a market which has clear subdivisions,
(*c*) advantage to be gained from the establishment of some form of price-fixing agreement, as in the case of a cartel.
(*d*) a seasonal change in demand conditions.

The question also calls for some knowledge of fixed and variable costs incurred by airlines and how these may be related to marginal cost pricing policy.

The plan for the answer is:

1   Show the benefits of the International Air Transport Association and how it enabled joint maximisation of profits for its members.

2   Show how there are virtually two distinct markets for air travel
and how this is likely to affect pricing policies.
3   Comment on the cost structure of an airline and how this affects
pricing policies.
4   Comment on the logical outcome of Pan Am's decisions.

SUGGESTED ANSWER

The type of competitive situation is the key to the economic rationale
which is described in the question. For many years the major airlines
of the world consulted with each other on matters of policy through
their membership of IATA (International Air Transport Association).
This organisation acted as a cartel since the member airlines agreed on
scales of fares, flight frequencies and flight capacities for passengers on
the regular routes operated between member countries. These
arrangements were encouraged (or, at least, not actively opposed) by
governments. It was held that such arrangements would ensure
adequate profits, adequate services to passengers and high standards of
safety. They would also go some way to ensuring the recovery of the
large investments which airlines should make in new aircraft.
Therefore, prior to the appearance in the market of Laker, there was
an orthodox oligopoly in air transport across the North Atlantic and
in this market Pan Am was the recognised leader. Pan Am and its
fellow IATA members could therefore follow a policy of common
fixed prices and joint profit maximisation. Demand for seats on
transatlantic flights is markedly seasonal and Laker was attracted to
enter the market initially because of the excess demand by tourists
during the holiday season. By eliminating some of the extra in-flight
services offered by the established airlines and making economies in
the sale of tickets and other areas of administration, Laker was able to
reduce his costs per passenger-mile and so initiate a price war. Once
this happened it was necessary for his competitors to retaliate to retain
their market share. In this way the original competitors found their
profits shrinking or even disappearing because the cuts made in their
fares could not quickly be matched by cost reductions.
   A study of the cost structure of a typical airline would be likely to
show that fixed costs are extremely high in relation to variable costs.
Once an airline is committed to flying a scheduled service the only
costs which are really variable are those for fuel and in-flight
consumables (food and drink). The addition to these costs per
passenger flown is so small that marginal cost per passenger is nearly
zero. The data given in the question shows that profits depend on
filling more than half the seats on any given flight. Airlines know that
there are, broadly speaking, two markets for these seats, (a) the

business travel market (price-inelastic demand rules here), and (b) the leisure travel market, where demand is very price-elastic. It is not, therefore, surprising that the airlines are willing to offer some seats at reduced prices in the latter market. How many seats are offered and their prices clearly depend on the seasonal changes in demand.

When Laker first entered the industry other airlines were prepared to tolerate his low fares at times of peak demand, but at other times Laker was a serious threat to the cartel. His rivals probably hoped that low-season demand would undermine Laker sooner rather than later. Laker responded to the winter fall in demand from tourists by attempting to win business travellers from his rivals through the introduction of the Regency Class mentioned in the question. If successful, this would have made a contribution to his high fixed costs of maintenance at all seasons, but would have weakened his rivals' profitability and reduced their cash flows.

The response of Pan Am and others was to cut fares to such levels that Laker (with far smaller resources of capital) would be unable to match them and stay in business. This explains the use of the word 'predatory' since a predator is one who kills. Once it had succeeded in ousting Laker, the way would be clear for the cartel to raise prices and recover losses. Such conduct may fall foul of legislation designed to protect consumers from the abuse of monopoly power and in this case led to legal action by Laker in the American courts which have often ruled against price-fixing agreements.

QUESTION 3—VERTICAL INTEGRATION

The following passage is adapted from a report in *The Guardian*, 23 October 1979.

'Audiotronics Ltd is an electronics distributing group which sold off the famous but loss-making Lasky Hi-Fi retail chain to Ladbroke for over £3 million. (Ladbroke had no previous connections with Hi-Fi retailing.) Audiotronics can now look forward to a profitable future, it imports and distributes a range of industrial and consumer electronic goods. It can now expand overseas operations and expects to purchase another UK wholesale electronics distributor. The sale of the former Lasky retail chain has brought profits as former retail competitors are now willing to purchase supplies from Audiotronics Ltd.'

(a) Comment on the disadvantages of vertical integration.
(b) Why might a company be willing to buy a chain of loss-making shops?

[*June 1981, London*]

NOTES ON ANSWERING THE QUESTION

Part (a) first requires a definition of the term used in the question: vertical integration. The disadvantages to be discussed can be categorised into those which can be inferred from the question (bearing in mind that it is about the wholesaler/retailer relationship) and those of a more general kind which could apply to any vertical integration. It is also possible to distinguish disadvantages to the firm itself and those which affect much wider sections of the community.

Part (b) should start by defining the type of merger represented by the Ladbroke take-over of Lasky's. In explaining why a loss-making chain of shops may be bought by a company, reference must first be made to the reasons likely to apply in the case quoted. Some knowledge of the operations in which Ladbroke's was already engaged is required, but since this firm is well known for its activities in the leisure industry this should not be a major difficulty for most candidates. As in part (a) the answer should then be developed to quote reasons which might apply both in the case where the purchase results in a vertical integration and where it results in a horizontal integration. In this part of the answer, references to particular actual cases are likely to earn additional marks.

SUGGESTED ANSWER

(a) Vertical integration occurs when a firm at one stage of production takes over or merges with another at a later stage (forward vertical integration), or at an earlier stage (backward vertical integration). In this case both Audiotronics and Lasky's may have felt that reliance upon each other in a supplier/outlet relationship was resulting in a failure to earn maximum profits. Lasky's may have been more profitable had it been able to buy a wider range of other products from other distributors. In turn, other distributors may have been reluctant to buy from Audiotronics, fearing that if supplies of products became short Lasky's would always receive more favourable treatment. If this were true these other firms would be disadvantaged. If any of their retail outlets then had to be closed the community would be at a disadvantage through a reduction of choice and competition. In any large vertical integration dis-economies of scale arise sooner or later. Bureaucracy increases, co-ordination of the different departments becomes more difficult and problems of communication occur, all of which increases costs and erodes profit margins. The interdependence of one part of the business upon another means that any breakdown at one stage affects all others in a chain reaction.

Thus, vertical integrations are particularly exposed to the risk of strikes. It is also likely that as the firm grows bigger the possibilities of further internal economies of scale will become less and less. In this case, with only Lasky's as a retail outlet, the scope for quantity discounts on purchases made by Audiotronics would be limited. By switching to a horizontal form of expansion Audiotronics would be able to extend the advantages from bulk buying.

(*b*) The take-over by Ladbrokes is a lateral integration where firms join together which are in the same stage of production (tertiary in this case), but are involved with quite different products. Such mergers form a conglomerate business.

Ladbroke's is a company which originated in the gambling industry and then extended into hotels and real estate (it owns at least one race-course). These activities are concerned with leisure time use and so are sales of hi-fi equipment. It is possible that Ladbroke's management believed that it could turn Lasky's losses into profits by adopting better techniques of control, management and publicity. Much would depend on the locations of Lasky's shops. Some might be in areas where they could more profitably be converted into betting shops. Others could be sold to other types of retail organisation at prices in excess of their balance sheet valuations, thus providing Ladbroke's with a capital gain. Yet another possibility is that Ladbroke's felt that their existing interests were already maximising profits and so diversification into a new area might be a safeguard against declining demand in their original activities. Where vertical integrations in retailing occur, a wholesaler or manufacturer may buy loss-making shops in order to secure a more effective presentation of his products and so obtain a larger share of the market. He may also think it possible to achieve economies of scale, particularly in transport costs. Horizontal integrations on the other hand are often aimed at the elimination of competing outlets and the establishment of greater control over retail prices.

QUESTION 4—SOCIAL COSTS

It has been argued that the entire cost of modifying the design of new cars in order to meet the requirements of anti-pollution legislation should be met by the car manufacturers on the grounds that such costs are simply one of the costs of doing business. The manufacturers, however, point out that they are not able to recover fully these costs by means of higher prices. Consequently, company profits will suffer, leading to redundancies and even, perhaps, to the bankruptcy of some of the smaller manufacturers of specialist cars.

(*a*) Outline the social costs which may result from (i) the ownership and operation of cars and (ii) the implementation of anti-pollution legislation.

(b) Under what conditions, if any, might a government subsidy towards the additional costs incurred by the manufacturers be reasonable? (If you think that a subsidy should not be provided, explain your opinion.)

[*January 1978, London*]

NOTES ON ANSWERING THE QUESTION

This question has relevance both to micro-economics and to macro-economics. The former is indicated by reference to 'costs of doing business' and 'company profits will suffer'. The latter is indicated a little less directly by the references to redundancies and the concept of social costs. In part (b) discussion needs to be widened to take an international view and not simply a domestic view. It is also important to note that in part (b) the inference is that a definite stance needs to be taken on the desirability or otherwise of giving a subsidy. There are two reasons for saying this:

(i) the question does not ask for the cases for *and* against subsidies,
(ii) to state both views not only ignores this fact, it also wastes valuable time.

The plan for the answer is:

Part (a)
1 Define concisely 'social cost'.
2 Give examples of social costs, indicating whether they are easily quantifiable or not.
3 Consider price elasticity of demand for cars bearing in mind that there is a division of the market into different groups of buyers.
4 Consider supply/demand conditions for substitutes for cars.

Part (b) Whichever view is taken about subsidies the answer needs to cover the short and long run with regard to:

1 Consequences for employment.
2 Consequences for balance of trade/payments.
3 Consequences for taxation and the PSBR.
4 Consequences for some social costs.

SUGGESTED ANSWER

(a)(i) A social cost is a cost imposed on the community at large, or on a significant section of the community, by the actions of an individual or a group.

The ownership and operation of cars imposes a variety of social costs. The most apparent is the cost of accidents which involve the community in the costs of treating those people who are injured and of repairing damage to property, to say nothing of the loss of production which occurs because of death or personal injury, and time wasted when other vehicles are delayed. A further significant cost arises from noise and air pollution. The former may necessitate expense on sound insulation of buildings and more frequent redecoration as paint work deteriorates, or it may entail loss of efficiency in working. The latter leads to a shorter life expectancy and the costs of treating various diseases arising from polluted air. Less quantifiable are the costs of traffic congestion which may increase the costs of distributing goods, and the effects of vibration on the structure of buildings.

(ii) Anti-pollution policies have costs for the community as well as benefits. These measures increase the costs of production of cars and will lead to higher prices if profit margins are to be protected. The consequences for employment in firms engaged in the motor industry depend on the price elasticity of demand for cars. If this is price elastic, car sales will fall significantly and employees will be laid off or made redundant. This is likely to occur where private motorists are the buyers, but demand may be less price elastic where the buyers are firms which need fleets of cars for their employees. The decrease in demand for cars would be even more marked if anti-pollution devices caused an increase in the running costs of cars. Fitting such devices also entails an opportunity cost for the community since resources devoted to the modification of existing cars and/or fuel could not be utilised in other ways.

Any reduction in car ownership and use would cause an increase in demand for public transport. The benefits of anti-pollution measures would then need to be weighed against the costs involved in providing more public transport. These costs could be considerable if they entailed the sort of capital outlay involved in such projects as the Victoria Line of London Transport.

(b) (*Alternative answers are given here since the candidate may agree or disagree with the idea of subsidies in this case.*)
In favour of a subsidy it may be argued that by softening the blow of higher production costs the price rises on cars would be less, hence maintaining demand for cars and the labour used in their production. The alternative might be some form of state ownership, which free enterprisers would deplore. Assuming that manufacturers do not absorb any extra costs imposed by anti-pollution measures, a subsidy would be justified if the social benefits are deemed to exceed the costs of the subsidy and any other social costs. Social benefits and social

costs are often hard to quantify, but more quantifiable benefits would be the lower costs of the health service and the lower costs of maintenance of roads and buildings. It can also be argued that the manufacture of devices controlling pollution could promote the growth of new small businesses and create new jobs. Lastly, the subsidy may enable the domestic car industry to compete effectively with foreign manufacturers so producing beneficial effects on domestic employment and the balance of payments.

OR

Against the subsidy it may be argued that it would constitute a new burden on the public purse which would need additional revenue to cover it. This could come from an increase in taxation or the PSBR. A possible increase in taxation would be a higher Road Fund Licence Fee or a higher oil/petroleum duty. Other things remaining the same, car owners/operators would have to economise on other spending or reduce their savings ratios. If income tax were increased, the fall in disposable income would reduce demand for less essential commodities, so that providers in these areas would effectively be providing the subsidy by a fall in their profits. Alternatively, it can be argued that the net result of a subsidy would be that car buyers would benefit at the expense of those who do not buy cars. Market forces would not be allowed to operate freely and a misallocation of resources would follow. An increase in the PSBR may be considered by monetarists to be inflationary, and some people would say that consumers of privately-owned means of transport should pay the full economic cost of this privilege. Should the government not wish to increase taxation or the PSBR it would be necessary to cut state spending in other directions.

QUESTION 5—MINIMUM WAGES

'A minimum wage would not really help the poorest families because, of those in the bottom 10% of the earnings distribution, only 20% are in the bottom 10% of the household income distribution.'

Discuss the factors that might explain this result.
[*January 1982, London*]

NOTES ON ANSWERING THE QUESTION

Although many questions about minimum wages have a distinct bias to micro-economics in terms of the theory of the market this question is much more concerned with macro-economic points.

Successful answers will need to demonstrate some practical knowledge of the way in which the social security system operates in the UK. Answers also need to distinguish between two key concepts which appear in the question, namely 'earnings distribution' and 'income distribution'.

The plan for the answer is:

1   Distinguish between earnings and income.
2   Show the types of people for whom a minimum wage would be irrelevant.
3   Show the types of people for whom a minimum wage would be relevant.
4   Explain the so-called poverty trap and show why marginal wage increases do not necessarily increase total income.

SUGGESTED ANSWER

Earnings distribution is a term that does not cover the whole population since it refers only to individuals in employment. It therefore excludes those incomes that are derived from other sources. The household income distribution covers all forms of income, but instead of referring to individuals it applies to groups of people who live together as a family unit.

People who are in the bottom 10 per cent of household income distribution include many of the unemployed, the physically and mentally handicapped, the retired and the vast majority of children. None of these categories would be included in the earnings distribution and their members are likely to derive significant amounts of income from various transfer payments. Some may receive small amounts of interest in their incomes but the total involved is likely to be very small. From these facts it can be seen that a minimum wage is largely irrelevant for these people.

Those in the bottom 10 per cent of the earnings distribution are likely to live in higher density housing because such people are often members of large, or extended families. Such families will usually have more than one income and may not, therefore, be included in the bottom 10 per cent of the household income distribution.

Attention also needs to be given to those just above the bottom 10 per cent of earnings distribution. Significant numbers of these may live alone in rented accommodation and are regarded, therefore, as a household. Their income could well be low enough to put them in the bottom 10 per cent of the household income distribution. It is this group which might be expected to gain from a minimum wage policy. There are also people on low earnings who also receive transfer payments which are sufficient to lift their families above the bottom 10 per cent of the household distribution table. This applies to families with many children or where there are aged relatives to support.

It might be assumed at first sight that a minimum wage policy would help these families who are regarded as the poorest in society. This is not so because of the way the social security and taxation systems work in the UK. The rules of these systems create the so-called poverty trap. As earned income rises for these families they eventually have their social security payments reduced. For instance, rent and heating allowances are reduced and entitlement to free school meals for children is lost. If the increase in earnings is enough, the recipient may find that gross income has exceeded the maximum which gives exemption from income tax. Together, the loss of social security benefits and the payment of income tax may mean that for each additional pound earned more than this is lost. If this is the case, a minimum wage would certainly not help these families. To give any improvement in their circumstances the minimum wage would have to be high, to more than offset the loss of social benefits and any liability for income tax occasioned by the families' higher money income. If the minimum wage were set this high it could have the effect of reducing the demand for labour, so making for more unemployment and more families in the lower levels of income distribution.

QUESTION 6—NORTH SEA OIL AND GAS

Table 1   Income from oil and gas production
(Details may not add to totals owing to roundings)

		£ Billion, 1978 prices 1980
1	Value of oil and gas production	6.6
2	Goods and services bought outside the sector	0.6
3	Value-added by North Sea sector (item 1 minus item 2) of which	5.9
3a	Total royalties plus pre-tax profits	5.8
3b	Employment income	0.1
4	Interest, profits and dividends due abroad	1.4
5	GNP at market prices arising within the sector (item 3 minus item 4)	4.5
6	Total GNP at market prices*	225.6

Table 2:   Balance of payments contributions: North Sea oil and gas
(Details may not add to totals due to rounding)

		£ Billion at 1978 prices
		1980
1	Oil and gas production, at equivalent import values	8.8
2	Net imports of goods and services less exports of some services directly for the programme	0.6
3	Interest, profit and dividends due overseas	1.4
4	Net contribution to the current account (item 1 minus item 2 minus item 3)	6.8
5	Net effect on capital account	+0.5
6	Net identified effect on the balance for official financing (item 4 plus item 5)	7.3
7	Current account balance★	+3.1
8	Total capital transactions on the balance of payments★	−1.4

Table 3:   Government Revenues from North Sea

		£ Billion at out-turn prices
		1979/1980
1	Royalties	0.52
2	Petroleum Revenue Tax	0.73
3	Corporation Tax	0.14
4	Total North Sea Revenues (item 1 plus item 2 plus item 3)	1.39
5	Total central government tax revenues	73.9

★ 1980 prices
Source: *Economic Progress Reports*

(*a*) What were the main ways in which North Sea oil and gas affected the UK balance of payments in 1980?   (*4 marks*)
(*b*) Are the figures in the tables directly comparable? Give reasons for your answer.   (*2 marks*)
(*c*) Discuss the significance of North Sea oil and gas to the UK economy.   (*14 marks*)

NOTES ON ANSWERING THE QUESTION

This question gives in tabular form data which the candidate is expected to interpret in the context of relevant economic theory and current economic affairs.

Part (*a*) is straightforward and merely requires a brief analysis of the data given in Table 2. For example, oil and gas production valued at £8.8 billion represents visible exports and savings on import expenditure.

Part (*b*) requires acknowledgement that constant price data is not being used, i.e. inflation compounds the problems of comparison.

Part (*c*) is the most interesting part of the question. It asks for an *assessment* of the importance of North Sea oil and gas to the UK economy. A good answer will be stimulated by the data given in the tables, although it can be used to introduce a wider discussion. The tables provide statistics on the contributions to the GNP, balance of payments and government revenues. In isolation, these are not very informative and need to be assessed with reference to total GNP, the current account balance and total capital transactions on the balance of payments. These figures serve as benchmarks. For example, the relative importance of the North Sea to total GNP can be ascertained by calculating the production of the former as a percentage of the latter. Two per cent represents a relatively small contribution. Similar calculations reveal that North Sea oil as a source of tax revenue is not very significant compared with total central government income, but its contribution to the balance of payments is considerable.

General conclusions deduced from the data can be qualified with knowledge that is not necessarily contained in the tables. In assessing the importance of the North Sea to GNP, comment could be made on the opportunity cost of resources invested in exploration and extraction, which obviously reduces its significance. Conversely, expertise which British companies have developed as a result of activities in the North Sea has been exported, and increased earnings from invisibles add to its significance for the balance of payments.

Other possible areas of discussion include the spin-off effects, such as less reliance on OPEC, and the controversy surrounding the uses to which North Sea revenues have been put.

SUGGESTED ANSWER

(*a*) The effect of North Sea oil and gas on the balance of payments current account is made up of three elements. First, there is oil and gas production valued at £8.8 billion which represents visible exports and savings on import expenditure. Second, there are imports of related goods and services such as rigs, platforms and contractors. These can be set against similar exports developed in recent years, although there is still a net loss of £0.6 billion. Third, there are the interest, profits and dividends of foreign companies operating in the North Sea. These constitute invisible imports amounting to £1.4 billion. On the capital account there is a net inflow of £0.5 billion which arises out of foreign investment in the North Sea and the finance of British companies with loans from abroad. Overall, North Sea oil and gas result in a £7.3 billion credit on the UK balance of payments.

(*b*) Care must be taken in comparing the figures in the three tables because Tables 1 and 2 are mostly expressed in 1978 prices while Table 3 gives 1979/80 prices. Furthermore, totals for GNP, the current account balance and capital transactions are expressed in 1980 prices. Consequently the money values contained in Table 3 and these totals will be higher than those of Tables 1 and 2 due to the effects of inflation. This hampers comparison in real terms.

(*c*) The contribution of North Sea oil and gas to the GNP is relatively small at $(4.5/225.6) \times 100 = 2$ per cent. The net addition is likely to be even smaller since resources used in the North Sea may have been utilised to increase production elsewhere in the economy, i.e. there is an opportunity cost involved. Furthermore, employment arising out of North Sea extraction is minor, since the production of oil and gas is an extremely capital intensive activity.

North Sea oil also makes a contribution to the economy as an additional source of revenue. The tax revenues help to stabilise the public sector borrowing requirement and can be used to finance increases in public expenditure or tax reductions in other areas. The extra revenue should, however, be put in perspective. The £1.39 billion raised constitutes only 1.88% of total central government revenue; less than that raised from indirect taxes on petrol and other oil products.

There is, however, another source of government revenue arising indirectly out of North Sea oil and gas: the profits of BP, the British National Oil Corporation and British Gas. State holdings in these organisations were in 1980 46 per cent, 100 per cent and 100 per cent respectively (currently 31.7 per cent, 44 per cent and 100 per cent). Their profits also help to reduce the PSBR.

The most significant effect is on the balance of payments. The net surplus on capital transactions relating to North Sea oil and gas not only helped to finance the overall deficit, but also represented additional investment in the UK economy. Moreover the net contribution of North Sea oil and gas made possible a surplus of £3.1 billion on the current account which would otherwise have been in deficit. It should not, however, be assumed that without North Sea products the current account deficit would have been £3.7 billion. One of the effects of North Sea oil and gas was to strengthen the external value of the pound. Without North Sea oil a devaluation of sterling could have been expected which would have resulted in more non-oil exports. A further qualification needs to be made in assessing North Sea contributions to the balance of payments: interest, profits and dividends due overseas constituted 15.9 per cent of all oil and gas production in 1980. This represents a substantial proportion.

Since becoming a major supplier of oil to the EEC, the UK's bargaining position within the Community has strengthened and this may have been relevant to negotiations, particularly those concerning budget contributions and receipts. Additional benefits for the balance of payments arise out of the export of products and expertise which British companies have developed as a result of activities in the North Sea. The UK is now less reliant on oil imports from Saudi Arabia and other OPEC countries, but this advantage may be partially offset by a reduction in their ability or willingness to purchase UK exports.

When considering the importance of North Sea oil and gas, indirect effects on the rest of UK industry should also be taken into account and these are not revealed by the statistics. The benefits of the North Sea obscure structural weaknesses and lack of price competitiveness in the economy. At present oil and gas revenues are being used to finance the non-oil balance of payments deficit and welfare benefits paid to the unemployed resulting from uncompetitive manufacturing industry in contraction. Alternatively, gas and oil revenues could be used for investment in manufacturing industry and this represents a long-term remedy. It has been estimated that within 20 years, the UK will become a net importer of oil again as reserves run out. During the intervening period the tax revenue and balance of payments surplus could be used to restructure the UK's manufacturing base in order to produce goods for export and domestic consumption at competitive prices. This is a permanent solution to problems of slow growth, unemployment and current account deficits and is thought by many economists to be the real importance of North Sea oil and gas to the UK economy.

QUESTION 7—STERLING M3 AND THE RETAIL PRICE INDEX

(a) Specify the items included in Sterling M3.   (3 marks)

(b) Describe the relationship between the Retail Price Index and Sterling M3 in the United Kingdom between 1965 and 1980.
                                                                    (5 marks)

(c) Discuss the significance of the data in the context of recent controversy about the causes of inflation.   (12 marks)

[*November 1983, AEB*]

The annual rate of change of the Retail Price Index
and the money supply (Sterling M3) for the United Kingdom 1965–80

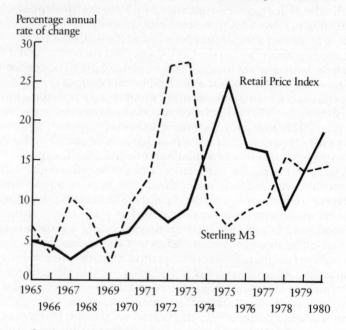

Source: *Economic Trends*

NOTES ON ANSWERING THE QUESTION

The question displays data in graphic form and concerns the
relationship between the growth rate of Sterling M3 and the rate of
increase in prices. The economic theory relevant to the question has its
basis in the Fisher equation: $MV = PT$, where M = money supply,
V = velocity of circulation, P = price level, and T = total number of
transactions (output). This is an undeniable identity. If the total
amount of money in existence is multiplied by the speed at which it
passes from one person to another, MV is equal to total goods and
services bought by consumers in a given period of time. Similarly,
total transactions multiplied by their average price is also equal to total
spending in a given time period. Therefore, MV is necessarily equal to
PT.

In the original 'quantity theory of money' the link between the
money supply and prices is immediate, with velocity and output
remaining stable. However, modern monetarists concede that

reductions in the rate of growth of the money supply will have a short-term effect on output and employment during the process of adjustment. The velocity of circulation tends to be constant throughout, so that once output returns to equilibrium level, changes in the rate of money supply growth are transmitted to changes in the rate of inflation. Friedman claims that the time lag involved is about 2 years.

Part (*a*) demands a straightforward definition which is given in the answer which follows. Part (*b*) asks for a description of the relationship between the Retail Price Index and the government's main target, Sterling M3. The figures are not consistent with the view that money supply growth has an immediate effect on inflation, but do provide evidence of a lagged correlation during the 1970s.

Part (*c*) involves interpretation of details summarised in part (*b*). The controversy about the causes of inflation centres on the differences between monetarist and Keynesian models. First of all, it is necessary to examine the monetarist view that inflation is a monetary phenomenon with reference to the data provided. Keynesians interpret the statistics differently. While not denying that a correlation exists, the money supply is seen as a passive rather than an active variable. Success in reducing the rate of inflation through restrictive monetary policy is explained as the inevitable result of further deflation at a time of world recession. The Keynesian model uses an 'institutional' approach to account for increases in the price level, e.g. trade union strength in the 1960s and the formation of OPEC in the 1970s.

SUGGESTED ANSWER

(*a*) Sterling M3 is composed of notes and coins in circulation plus all bank deposits which are denominated in sterling.

(*b*) The figures for Sterling M3 and the retail price index converge in some years and diverge in others. For example, between 1967 and 1969 the annual rate of change in Sterling M3 decreased while the rate of change in the retail price index increased, displaying an inverse relationship. Conversely, between 1969 and 1971 they both increased, so that the figures displayed a direct relationship. However, from a monetarist perspective the relationship between Sterling M3 and the rate of inflation is lagged. A change in the rate of growth of Sterling M3 will be reflected in the rate of inflation approximately 2 years later. The figures between 1965 and 1970 do not provide any clear-cut evidence for this claim, but it is consistently supported by the figures for the 1970s. Between 1971 and 1972, the rate of growth in

Sterling M3 increased from 13 to 27 per cent. This relates to the rate of inflation between 1973 and 1974 which increased from 8 to 24 per cent. When the rate of growth in Sterling M3 fell between 1973 and 1974, there was a corresponding fall in the inflation rate between 1975 and 1976.

(*c*) A positive correlation between two variables does not prove cause and effect, and much of the recent controversy about the causes of inflation revolves around the differences in interpretation of the statistics.

Monetarists argue that inflation is mainly—if not entirely—a monetary phenomenon. Evidence for this view is provided by the figures between 1970 and 1980 where a rise in Sterling M3 at a given point in time is linked to a rise in the retail price index 2 years later. Monetarists claim, therefore, that price rises are only possible if the rate of growth in money supply is allowed to accommodate them. For the monetarists, external shocks such as the oil price rises in the early 1970s are, in isolation, largely irrelevant to the inflationary process. Although rapid increases in all prices ensued, they were financed by increases in the money supply. The oil price rises could have been contained, rather than allowed to spread to other goods and services, if governments had controlled the rate of growth in the money supply.

This monetarist interpretation of the data has been criticised by Keynesian economists who argue that the money supply is a 'passive' rather than an 'active' variable. Keynesians claim that Sterling M3 is a residual which adjusts to changes in output and inflation rates rather than the other way round. In other words, the causal chain is reversed with changes in the money supply reflecting, not activating the rate of inflation.

In contrast to the monetarist view, this approach emphasises external shocks to the economy as the major causes of inflation. For example, the rise in prices during the late 1960s can be explained by an increase in trade union militancy. Similarly, the rapid surge in the rate of inflation between 1973 and 1975 is explained by the oil price rise. The rate of monetary growth merely changes to accommodate the new level of prices and changes in aggregate demand. (For a more informed assessment of the alternative theory, figures on changes in output over the same period would be required.)

Contractions in output and employment are considered by Keynesians to be the only real effects of a restrictive monetary policy. Attempts to control money supply through high interest rates and reductions in the PSBR are deflationary and lead to a fall in aggregate demand. To further deflate the economy at a time of world recession will inevitably cause the rate of inflation to decrease. This has more to do with decreases in aggregate demand than control of money supply.

Both schools of thought regard wage rates as a key element in the inflationary process. The fall in the rate of increase in average earnings has been instrumental in bringing about a deceleration in the inflation rate during the early 1980s. Monetarists explain moderated wage demands as a response to reduced inflationary expectations. Keynesians view lower pay settlements as a result of union power weakened by recession and a reaction to the fear of unemployment. Similarly, firms are compelled to cut profit margins.

Opponents of monetary policy account for the fall in the inflation rate experienced between 1980 and 1983 as the outcome of deflationary policies at a time of world recession combined with lower import prices resulting from the relatively high value of sterling and a reduction in commodity prices. While a tight monetary policy can succeed in deflating the economy and bringing about falls in output, employment and the rate of price increases, it does little to tackle the root causes of inflation.

The controversy about the link between money supply and inflation mainly concerns the transmission mechanism. That is, whether control of monetary growth transmits to the rate of inflation or whether prices and output transmit to money supply. The data can be used in support of either interpretation.

3

Markets

QUESTION 1—EXPENDITURE ON ALCOHOLIC DRINK

Consumers' Expenditure on Alcoholic Drink
(£ million, quarterly at 1970 prices)

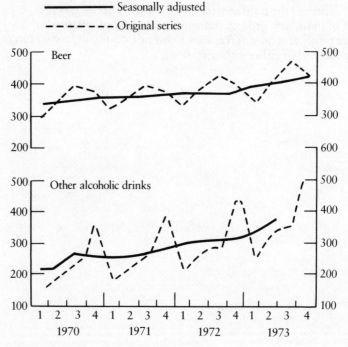

(Adapted from the Treasury's *Economic Progress Report*, HMSO, March 1975)

(*a*) What factors could help to account for the pattern of consumers' expenditure on alcoholic drink, as shown in the diagram?

26

(*b*) What advantages do seasonally-adjusted figures of expenditure have over non-adjusted figures?

[*June 1977, London*]

SUGGESTED ANSWER

(*a*) Seasonal factors are largely responsible for the changes shown in the original series line in each graph. For example, peak beer consumption is always associated with the third quarter of the year (which is usually the quarter of holidays and highest temperatures). On the other hand, sales of beer reach their lowest in the first quarter of each year when few people take a holiday in Britain and temperatures are at their lowest. Other alcoholic drinks reach peak sales in the last quarter of each year when, by tradition, such drinks are associated with the celebration of Christmas and the New Year. Sales of these drinks then decline sharply with the return to work in January and the arrival of annual bills of various kinds which consumers must pay. However, it is noticeable that on both graphs each peak and each lowest point occur at higher levels every year. This may indicate that each year produced a rising real income for consumers.

Had these figures not been converted to 1970 prices the consumption increases would have seemed even more pronounced because of rising prices associated with inflation. Putting this point in another way, alcoholic drinks became cheaper in real terms during the years mentioned in the question. This produced a positive real income effect for consumers. A substitution effect is also disclosed by the graphs which show modest increases in beer consumption when compared with that of other alcoholic drinks.

Wine is still considered by many to be a luxury good. The fact that consumption of wine increased significantly is because: (*a*) real incomes were rising—so more luxuries could be afforded; (*b*) a social change was under way—the middle classes were substituting wine drinking at home for visits to public houses; (*c*) the increases in indirect taxes on wine were not keeping pace with inflation; and (*d*) the period saw a reduction in working hours—more time was available for leisure and drinking.

The point about indirect taxes on all alcohol is worthy of closer examination. Taxes on wine were heavier than those on beer during this period; so, other things being equal, beer consumption should have risen more than wine consumption. The fact that it did not may have been a result of greater advertising of wines, particularly on television. So far as the general increase in consumption of alcohol is concerned, this could have been the result of an increase in the numbers of consumers over the age of 18 and the fact that UK membership of the EEC has brought a greater variety of drinks on to the market.

(*b*) Seasonally adjusted expenditure figures are better than non-adjusted ones because they reveal more accurately the underlying trends for a year or more. This sort of information enables producers to project future trends with more precision and, consequently, they can plan output and investment much more effectively. An example of such planning would be that of the size of the production unit required to deal with annual demand rather than maximum seasonal demand. Pursuing the latter course would leave a significant underutilisation of resources for most of the year (provided that the product is not perishable). Government planning could also benefit in this case by enabling the authorities to anticipate changes in tax yields.

In conclusion, producers and governments may wish to make comparisons of these statistics with those of other products, other countries and/or other time periods. If seasonal effects have been eliminated the comparisons will be more valid.

QUESTION 2—ENERGY PRICES AND MARKET SHARES

Market price data for rules used in the United Kingdom. 1965–75 (pence per therm).

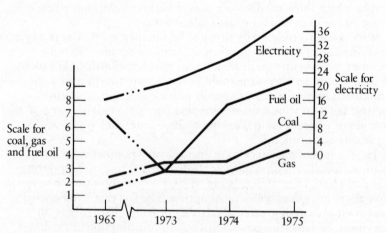

Energy consumed (billions of therms equivalent).

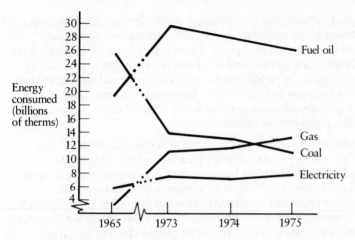

(Source: *Department of energy statistics*)

(*a*) What factors determine the relative prices of coal, gas, fuel oil and electricity?

(*b*) What explanations can you offer for the market shares and trends in consumption shown in these diagrams?

[*January 1980, London*]

SUGGESTED ANSWER

(*a*) The government is able to exercise considerable control over the prices of all these forms of energy either through its ownership of the industry (as in the cases of coal, gas and electricity) or through policies of taxation (as in the case of fuel oil). To a significant extent, all these sources of energy are substitutes for each other in the long run, and even in free market conditions their prices could be expected to move in the same general direction. However, the government can ensure by directives that, even in the short run, the prices do not differ markedly from each other. An example of this occurred in 1974 when the Gas Board was instructed to raise its prices to bring them more into line with those of the substitutes.

Demand always plays a part in price determination and is relatively stable in the energy market. It does not tend to bring about large relative changes, at least in the short run.

Supply has been much more variable than demand. Until the OPEC price rises imposed in 1973, North Sea gas prices had been falling as production was increased, but they rose slowly thereafter in sympathy with the big rise in fuel oil prices. The costs of production of these different forms of energy are by no means the same.

Coal, and natural gas (a by-product of oil), are primary products which do not incur manufacturing costs (although both require significant investments of capital). Electricity, on the other hand, does incur manufacturing costs, and is relatively expensive to produce. It should, of course, be noted that transport costs of coal are higher than those of fuel oil, gas and electricity. The two last named have extensive grid distribution systems in the UK, whereas coal is much more bulky per therm to transport.

(*b*) Price differences, especially in absolute terms, clearly affect the shares of the energy market taken by each product. This is best illustrated by the correlation between the fall in the price of gas up to 1973 and the higher levels of consumption which this induced. Relative price changes contribute to changes in market share through the substitution effect as was illustrated by the loss of market share by coal to oil from 1965 to 1973. The same period saw a switch from town gas (manufactured from coal) to cheaper natural gas as North Sea production developed. At this time there was considerable publicity given to the expected long-term price advantage of gas. Since the first OPEC oil price rise in 1973, oil and coal consumption have both declined in many cases while consumption of natural gas has increased. A comparison of the two graphs shows that despite the continually rising prices of electricity the quantity consumed has been remarkably constant. This inelasticity of demand for electricity is explained by the fact that for many uses—e.g. lighting and some chemical processes—there is no effective substitute.

Consumers of fuel are not only influenced by the cost of the fuel itself. They also have to consider the capital costs of the equipment for the consumption of the fuel, and these may be a significant deterrent in switching from one fuel to another, particularly for heating purposes. Householders do not readily replace oil-fired boilers by gas-fired boilers. Consumers consider reliability and availability of supplies and whether they need to have storage facilities for the fuel. In these respects, gas and electricity have advantages which enable them to retain, or even increase, their shares of the market. Finally, consumers prefer fuels for which there is reliability of price because this enables them to plan their budgets more effectively. Fuels are essential items and so price changes can have significant effects on other spending.

QUESTION 3—ELASTICITY OF SUPPLY

Peachville is a small town in the market of which growers sell their peaches (which is only one of their crops). The supply of peaches is totally inelastic on a given day as they have no storage or conserving facilities. They sell at an average retail price of 50p per kg, making an average profit of 4p per kg and an average weekly income from the peach crop of £30.

They consider these figures too low. The transport cost per kg to the nearest alternative market is 2p. Assume that if they increase their output it will be at constant average costs.

Discuss the alternative strategies open to them and what other information they should seek before choosing a strategy.

[*June 1980, London*]

SUGGESTED ANSWER

In the initial situation when profit is 4p per kg of peaches, the volume of sales required to earn a profit of £30 per week is 3,000/4 kg = 750 kg. Selling in the new market would add 2p per kg in transport costs; so the minimum acceptable price in this market would be 52p per kg. (This would equalise M.C. and M.R. for entry to this market.)

Short-run and long-run strategies need to be considered. In the short run there are two possibilities:

(*a*) Raising the price in Peachville.
(*b*) Selling at least part of the crop in the alternative market at a price higher than 52p per kg since a higher profit margin is the main objective.

A decision would require knowledge of the price elasticity of demand for peaches in Peachville. Unless this is less than unity any price increase would have the effect of lowering the volume of sales, and this could lead to even lower weekly incomes. It would also be necessary to find out some facts about the market conditions in the alternative market. Obviously the price elasticity of demand in that market is again of prime importance, as is the number of competitors and their costs of production. The growers would also wish to know if consumers in that market would be willing to buy from newcomers or whether they would stay loyal to their original suppliers. It would also be important to be aware of the quality of the product offered by competitors.

In the long run the following strategies may be considered:

(*a*) Reducing the area of land devoted to peach growing and substituting other more profitable crops;
(*b*) Setting up a canning plant;
(*c*) Allowing customers on to the land to pick their own peaches.

The growers would need to see projections of demand for peaches and the substitute crops—if these are available.

As peaches grow on trees, once the number of trees has been reduced it would take a considerable time before supply could be increased were demand for peaches to strengthen in the future. It might be possible to produce alternative crops within a year, but there would be little point in doing this if the market could not absorb the extra output without significant price reductions being made. The possibility of building and operating a canning factory would require consideration of the capital and revenue costs together with the availability of capital. One would also like to know whether any difficulties might arise over planning permission for the factory. Canning factories require large and continuous supplies of fruit if they are to operate efficiently and profitably. Information would, therefore, be necessary on the minimum economic throughput and the ability of the growers to provide this amount of fruit. It would also be desirable to consider the price fetched by canned peaches and how this might be affected by the establishment of a new supplier. There might also be difficulties in gaining access to wholesale and retail outlets.

QUESTION 4—HOUSING

1. Give a brief account of the changes in housing tenure illustrated by the pie-charts below. *(2 marks)*
2. What are the likely reasons for these changes? *(10 marks)*
3. 'There is a growing crude surplus of housing stock over households. This implies that supply deficiency in housing has been eliminated in the UK'. Discuss. *(8 marks)*

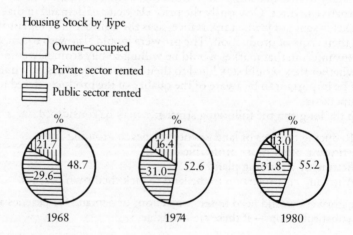

Housing Stock by Type

☐ Owner–occupied

▥ Private sector rented

▤ Public sector rented

| % | % | % |
| 1968 | 1974 | 1980 |

21.7 / 29.6 / 48.7 — 1968
16.4 / 31.0 / 52.6 — 1974
13.0 / 31.8 / 55.2 — 1980

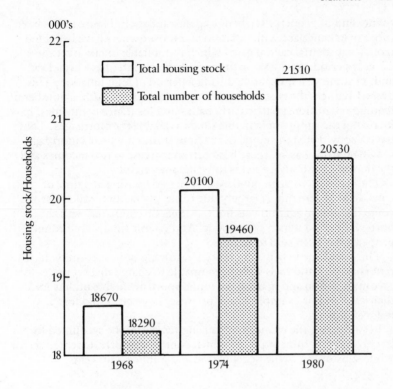

000's

Housing stock/Households

22 —

21 —

20 —

19 —

18 —

Total housing stock

Total number of households

1968   1974   1980

18670
18290
20100
19460
21510
20530

SUGGESTED ANSWER

(*a*) Taking the 12-year period as a whole, there has been a significant 6.5 per cent increase in owner-occupied tenure and a marginal increase of 2.2 per cent in public sector rented accommodation. These changes are balanced by a large decrease of 8.7 per cent in privately rented accommodation. In all three types of tenure, the degree of change was most marked in the first six year period 1968–74.

(*b*) The reasons for the increase in owner-occupied housing are many. First, there is empirical evidence of excess demand for both public and private rented accommodation. Lack of availability of rented property makes owner-occupiership the only viable alternative. Second, it has been government policy to sell council houses, particularly since 1979. Third, the government allows tax relief on mortgage interest for loans up to £30,000. This greatly reduces the cost of owner-occupiership and represents a government subsidy to the house buyer. Fourth, ownership of property is a hedge against inflation. House prices have more than kept pace with inflation and most owners have benefited from a substantial capital gain, which is not liable to tax, over the 12-year period. At the same time, real interest rates have been low and, in some years, negative during a period of high inflation. This greatly reduces the cost of borrowing in real terms. Fifth, a number of lending institutions, particularly banks and insurance companies, have increased the supply of loanable funds available for mortgages. They have also widened the range of schemes through which a mortgage may be repaid. Lastly, there has been an increase in real incomes and the demand for housing tends to be income-elastic.

The slight increase in public sector rented housing at a time of considerable demand, is largely due to supply factors. Much less council accommodation was built in 1968–80 compared with the post-war period which preceded it. At the same time, some council property has been sold to tenants.

The shrinkage in privately rented housing is almost entirely due to rent control. Landlords have been unable to charge market prices for accommodation and many have found more profitable outlets for their capital. For example, some premises have been sold for redevelopment.

In summary, the changes in housing tenure can be accounted for largely by government policy which controls the private rented sector while subsidising owner-occupation and public sector rents.

(*c*) The proposition that the emergence of a growing crude surplus of housing over households indicates that the United Kingdom no longer has a housing shortage is denied by the empirical evidence. The figures disguise a situation of excess demand for rented accommodation in both the public and private sectors. The statistics do not reveal information which might account for the surplus of housing units over households at a time when accommodation is in short supply.

As real incomes increase, some households may own more than one home and ownership of, for example, holiday bungalows, is becoming increasingly common. Ownership of more than one housing unit is also common among property speculators. Houses are often bought with the intention of making a capital gain and are likely to remain unoccupied in the intervening period. Similarly, there has been considerable controversy over unoccupied council properties awaiting renovation of slum clearance.

The statistics also fail to give details of location and type of housing. There may be a surplus of miners' cottages in South Wales but a shortage of mews cottages in central London. Similarly, there may be a surplus of flats in tower blocks but a shortage of suburban houses suitable for family occupation.

Finally, some individuals would have been assessed as members of a single household when ideally they would prefer to be part of a separate unit. These include married children currently living with parents and grandparents or single young people who might prefer studio flats of their own, given their availability and sufficient financial resources. Relatively expensive houses may also remain vacant since potential buyers cannot afford them.

For the large number of people who are anxious to buy or rent a property, the crude surplus of housing over households does not eliminate the problem of a shortage of suitable accommodation.

QUESTION 5—PRICE STABILITY IN THE SOVIET UNION

In the Soviet Union political expediency has involved the preservation of retail price stability over a long period of time. As a result Russians have been faced with rising subsidies in order to protect retail prices from the effects of rising costs. Several senior economists see dangers in doing this.

Consider the unfortunate outcome. The country is more prosperous now than it was 25 years ago and wages have risen in these years, but bread still being sold at 1958 prices is now so cheap in relation to incomes that it is frequently wasted. Rents, unchanged since 1928, make it almost impossible to maintain or improve residential property. Even energy prices are so low as not to encourage economy in its use.

People left with surplus purchasing power ignore the poor condition of their flats and usually buy basic necessities in bulk at low prices. Much of this consumption is wasteful and creates artificial shortages. At the same time consumers have enough spare cash to support black markets in imported and consumer goods.

Soviet economists would like to relieve the economy of the need to finance subsidies and in this way put industry on a more rational financial basis. A recent party congress outlined proposals to raise productivity, cut labour costs and use materials more efficiently. One could almost hear the cry 'The economy must be economical'.

Refer specifically to the passage above and explain how the centrally planned economy faces problems not encountered in a market economy.

SUGGESTED ANSWER

In the market economy the price system performs important functions. Changes in the taste and/or quantitative requirements of consumers are communicated to producers by those consumers offering higher or lower prices for commodities. Changes in the costs of inputs are reflected in higher or lower prices charged by producers. Prices which are free to fluctuate allow the fairly realistic determination of profit or loss in both the accounting and economic senses of the terms. This, in turn, determines the allocation of resources and the distribution of income. Furthermore, when prices are allowed to fluctuate in the domestic economy it is possible to make better informed decisions about imports from, and exports to, foreign countries. This is because world prices can be more accurately compared with domestic prices.

A state-planned economy, therefore, will have difficulty in dealing with changes in the world prices of essential imports. Russia often has to buy wheat on the world market where prices have risen considerably since 1958, but if domestic prices of bread are frozen at 1958 levels consumers will not realise the true value of bread. Waste in the use of bread will worsen the balance of payments position for Russia, and to pay for imported wheat a greater volume of production of other commodities will have to be diverted from the home market to the export trade.

In market economies governments can use the price mechanism to influence the level of demand for goods by means of subsidies and/or indirect taxes wherever it is thought that demand for the good is price elastic. Such measures may be used to stabilise demand and so give greater certainty to producers. If, however, frequent and/or large changes are made in these subsidies and taxes, demand will be destabilised and planning for the future will be made much less certain. This could have adverse effects upon investment programmes.

In the absence of an effective price system, decisions about what to produce and what levels of production to aim for must be taken centrally without the decision makers having at their disposal any clear market signals. Hence, if production is fixed at too low a level with regard to demand at a price set along ago, shortages will occur in shops. Planners must then institute some system of rationing or consumers must be prepared to queue. In either event, as the third paragraph of the article suggests, there will be a tendency for black markets to arise in which prices do hold sway.

Residential property in Russia is stated-owned. If rents are fixed at very low levels tenants will not have to plan their spending as carefully as they would in a free market. The state will find it necessary to subsidise maintenance of the property and will need to find another source of income to pay for this. Under the current system of planning in Russia planners try to estimate the production cost of a commodity. They also try to estimate a retail price. Any surplus of retail price over cost can be regarded as an indirect tax; any short-fall requires a subsidy. However, if retail prices are held constant and production costs increase, it is the tax yield that is affected rather than demand for the product. It is difficult to match tax income against expenditure on subsidies, but the wide use of subsidies makes it possible for production units to avoid reporting accounting losses.

The last paragraph of the passage refers to making the economy more efficient and creating a more realistic financial basis for industry. If, by 'efficient', the party means operating at the lowest possible averge total cost, the main problem will be to introduce realism into costs and prices so that they do reflect relative values and scarcity. If this is done, consumers must be made to accept (what is for them) a novel idea about prices, and the fact that forward planning may become more difficult and prone to error. The reduction of subsidies may also mean considerable changes in working practices in various undertakings and, more important still, considerable delegation of decision making from the centre to the regions of the economy in order to give full effect to regional cost differentials. Such changes involve some political re-education of society as well as economic re-education, and this may be the greatest problem faced by the state planners.

QUESTION 6—SUPPLY AND DEMAND

The data below relates to the demand for and supply of electronic components in the UK.

Supply and demand

Price (£s)	Demand per week (000's)	Supply per week (000's)
1	360	30
2	180	50
3	120	72
4	90	90
5	72	108
6	60	135

1. What will be the equilibrium price?
2. What is the price elasticity of demand?
3. What is the elasticity of supply around the price of £4?

Suppose that the supply schedule above represents the long-run situation and that demand for electronic components was to increase by 50 per cent at each price.

4. What would be the weekly sales and the price of electronic components in the short run:

(*a*) if producers meet the increased demand by supplying from stock at current prices?

(*b*) if there were no stocks and supply in the short run was perfectly inelastic?

(*c*) if the government imposed a maximum price of £8?

5. What would be the sales per week and equilibrium price in the long run?

6. In order to encourage consumption a subsidy of £2 for each component sold is introduced after the increase in demand previously mentioned.

What would be:

(*a*) the weekly sales and the price of electronic components?

(*b*) the total revenue of producers?

(*c*) the cost of the subsidy?

Explain your answers at each stage.

SUGGESTED ANSWER

1 The equilibrium price is £4.00. At this price supply is equal to demand.

2 Revenue remains constant at £360,000 at all prices.

The demand curve is, therefore, a rectangular hyperbola.

In this situation elasticity of demand is equal to unity.

3 Elasticity of supply $= \dfrac{\text{Proportionate change in quantity supplied}}{\text{Proportionate change in price}}$

$$= \frac{18/90}{1/4}$$

$$= \frac{0.2}{0.25}$$

$$= 0.8$$

4 The market for electronic components is now:

Price (£s)	Demand per week (000's)	Supply per week (000's)
1	$360 \times 1.5 = 540$	30
2	$180 \times 1.5 = 270$	50
3	$120 \times 1.5 = 180$	72

4	$90 \times 1.5 = 135$	90
5	$72 \times 1.5 = 108$	108
6	$60 \times 1.5 = 90$	135

(*a*) The weekly sales would be 135,000 units which is the new level of demand at the existing price of £4.00.

(*b*) If supply remains at 90,000 units per week, this level of sales will be absorbed with a price of £6.00.

(*c*) A maximum price of £8.00 would have no effect since this is above the equilibrium price.

5 The long-run equilibrium price is £5.00. At this price 108 units are supplied and demanded.

6 A subsidy of £2.00 will result in a shift in the supply curve. For example, the quantity previously supplied at £6.00 is now marketed at £4.00 since this price plus the subsidy provides the producer with the same income. In other words, there is a decrease in price of £2 for each quantity. The market for electronic components is now:

Price (£'s)	Demand per week (000's)	Supply per week (000's)
1	540	72
2	270	90
3	180	108
4	135	135
5	108	N/A
6	90	N/A

(*a*) The new level of sales is 135,000 units per week and the equilibrium price is £4.00.

(*b*) The revenue of producers for each unit sold is £2 in subsidy plus £4 market price, i.e. £6.

Total revenue = £6 × 135,000 = £810,000

(*c*) The cost of the subsidy = £2 × 135,000 = £270,000.

4

Forms of Competition

QUESTION 1—PROFIT MAXIMISATION

A publisher has to decide the price at which to sell a new book. He estimates that the costs incurred before publication amount to £10,000 and that variable costs amount to £1 a copy. In addition, he has agreed to pay the author royalties at a rate of 10 per cent of sales revenue. The publisher's best estimate of the number of books he would sell at different prices is as follows:

Price (£)	Number sold
1.00	60,000
1.25	40,000
1.50	35,000
1.75	20,000
2.00	10,000

(a) Which of the above prices would maximise the publisher's profits?
(b) Which of the above prices would maximise the author's royalties?
(c) Publishers often allow authors to suggest the names of people to whom free copies will be sent. In this instance the author has suggested 50 names. Experience suggests that for every free copy, three further copies are ordered at the normal price. Assuming that the publisher has set his profit maximising price without considering the question of free copies, should he try to persuade the author to increase/decrease his list?
(d) All the above data relate to a book published in black and white. The publisher estimates that publishing in colour would increase his variable costs by 25 per cent and demand by 20 per cent. How would his price be affected if he were to publish in colour instead of in black and white?

[June 1977, London]

SUGGESTED ANSWER

The publisher's profits are maximised at the price at which the difference between revenue and total costs is the greater.

Price (£)	×	Number sold	=	Revenue (£)
1.00		60,000		60,000
1.25		40,000		50,000
1.50		35,000		52,500
1.75		20,000		35,000
2.00		10,000		20,000

To calculate the total costs associated with each price:

Price (£)	Fixed costs (£)	+	Variable costs (£)	+	Royalties (£)	=	Total costs (£)
1.00	10,000		60,000		6,000		76,000
1.25	10,000		40,000		5,000		55,000
1.50	10,000		35,000		5,250		50,250
1.75	10,000		20,000		3,300		33,300
2.00	10,000		10,000		2,000		22,000

To calculate the profit associated with each price:

Price (£)	Revenue (£)	−	Total costs (£)	=	Profit (£)
1.00	60,000		76,000		−16,000
1.25	50,000		55,000		−5,000
1.50	52,500		50,250		+2,250
1.75	35,000		33,500		+1,500
2.00	20,000		22,000		−2,000

Therefore, the price which would maximise the publisher's profits is £1.50.

(*b*) For the author, marginal costs are zero. Therefore the author's royalties are maximised when revenue is maximised at price £1.00.
(*c*) The marginal cost is equal to the variable costs involved in producing four books plus the royalties earned on the sale of three books, i.e. £4.00 + 0.45p = £4.45. The marginal revenue is 3 × £1.50 = £4.50. Therefore each free copy appears to increase profits by 5p. This would, however, probably be swallowed up by postage, packing and administration costs. Under these circumstances the publisher is advised to persuade the author to decrease his list.
(*d*) Following the same method as in part (*a*):

Price (£)	×	Number sold	=	Revenue (£)
1.00		72,000		72,000
1.25		48,000		60,000
1.50		42,000		63,000
1.75		34,000		42,000
2.00		12,000		24,000

Price (£)	Fixed costs (£)	+	Variable costs (£)	+	Royalties	=	Total costs (£)
1.00	10,000		90,000	–	7,200		107,200
1.25	10,000		60,000	–	6,000		76,000
1.50	10,000		52,500	–	6,300		68,800
1.75	10,000		30,000	–	4,200		44,200
2.00	10,000		15,000	–	2,400		17,400

Price (£)	Revenue (£)	–	Total costs (£)	=	Profits (£)
1.00	72,000		107,200		−35,200
1.25	60,000		76,000		−16,000
1.50	63,000		68,800		− 5,800
1.75	42,000		44,200		− 2,200
2.00	24,000		27,400		− 3,400

If the publisher decides to print in colour he will find it impossible to make a profit. Losses will be minimised at a price of £1.75.

QUESTION 2—PERFECT AND IMPERFECT COMPETITION

'The classical theory of the firm relied heavily on the notion that firms are small owner-managed organisations operating in highly competitive markets whose demand functions are given and where only normal profits can be earned. If the firm did not therefore maximise profits it would fail to survive under those conditions. Setting aside the question as to whether this ever was a valid description . . . it is certainly far removed from the actual characteristics of firms in many branches of economic activity today. It is only when the main features of the organisation of modern corporations are taken into account that the questions of the goals of the firm and its decision processes can be effectively discussed.'

(J. F. Pickering, *Industrial Structure and Market Conduct*, Martin Robertson & Co. Ltd, 1974.)

(a) Explain, within the context of classical theory, how profit maximisation is crucial for a firm's survival.

(b) What 'main features of modern corporations' would you consider the author had in mind when he questioned the adequacy of the traditional theory of the firm? Giving your reasons, state whether you would agree that such theory is now obsolete.

[*January 1980, London*]

SUGGESTED ANSWER

(a) The term 'classical theory of the firm' is being used as a synonym for the theory of perfect competition. In perfectly competitive markets all firms in long-run equilibrium are marginal. Consequently, inefficient firms with high costs relative to their rivals are forced to leave the industry. As more productive competitors expand output and new firms enter the market, price will fall until the abnormal profits of the most efficient firms have been eliminated. At the same time, less efficient firms will have been priced out of the industry completely. Since price is outside the control of the individual firm, profit maximisation requires the lowest possible costs of production for any given output. Firms which fail to achieve minimum unit costs will incur losses and cease production in the long run. The diagram illustrates a perfectly competitive market. Firms with cost structure A are forced out of the market as supply increases in response to the abnormal profits being made by firms with cost structure B.

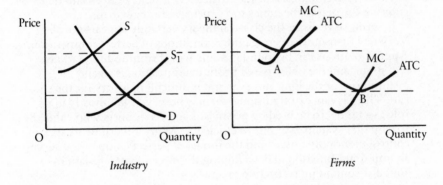

Industry   Firms

(b) The modern corporation is typified by the joint stock company which is increasingly multinational in its activities. It is characterised by a number of features which are in direct contrast with those assumed by the traditional theory of the firm. Markets are dominated by oligopolistic structures; firms are consequently large and there is a separation of management and control. Furthermore, the firm is able to determine the price of its good or service and maintain abnormal profits in the long run by erecting barriers to entry.

The assumption that all businesses in the private sector seek to maximise profits is questionable. While this may be true for the long run it need not apply to the short run while oligopoly is the market form. Firms frequently have short-run objectives which are not compatible with short-run profit maximisation. One such objective is market leadership achieved through sales (as opposed to profit) maximisation. A firm may also pursue policies aimed at the elimination of a competitor from the market. When a small rival appeared in the market for natural gases, British Oxygen conducted a policy of radical price cuts in the relevant area of the UK until the firm withdrew. In the long run, of course, BOC returned to profit-maximising prices. Similar price reduction tactics can be employed to force a rival to accept take-over terms.

Costs also affect profitability, but firms do not necessarily aim to minimise their outlay. Wage rates, for example, may be paid above the minimum in order to attract and retain better workers so that they are not tempted to take jobs with rivals. Such workers will not be laid off in the short run even though demand for the firm's product is slack. In addition, firms which employ workers in LDCs (Less Developed Countries) may choose to increase wages under pressure of public opinion, particularly if there is unfavourable publicity in the media. Costs are also raised by non-price competition, such as product differentiation and advertising. This policy can ensure that entering the market becomes too expensive for new firms.

In terms of realism, the classical theory certainly appears obsolete. Very few firms now operate under conditions of perfect competition. Approximations can be found in some world commodity markets, e.g. grain; and the objective of profit maximisation is a valid assumption for the long run even if it is difficult to justify for the short run. The relevance of traditional theory, however, lies mostly in its role as a model to be used by politicians and economists who value the free market system as a spur to efficiency. Many governments seek to control monopoly power and the model of perfect competition serves an important function in determining the direction of legislation aimed at containing restrictive practices.

QUESTION 3—COMPONENT COSTS

A firm estimates the cost schedules for the manufacture of one of its components as follows:

Quantity (00s)	Fixed costs (£)	Variable costs (£)
0	100	0
1	100	200
2	100	300
3	100	450
4	100	650
5	100	900

It believes its weekly requirements for this component will vary between 300 and 400. It receives an outside tender to supply any weekly number at a price of £1.00 each.

The firm, in fact, decides to continue manufacturing its own component.
Under what assumptions was this (a) a wise and (b) an unwise decision?

[*January 1981, London*]

SUGGESTED ANSWER

Calculations

Quantity 00s	AVC (£)
1	2.0
2	1.5
3	1.5
4	1.625
5	1.8

(a) On comparing the average variable costs as calculated above with the tender price of £1.00 per unit it seems to be wise to accept the tender, since this could open the way for higher profits and/or reduced prices to the consumer. In spite of this apparent advantage of accepting the tender there are good reasons for refusing it and continuing to manufacture the component.

It may be vital to exercise close control over the quality of the item and to be sure of its availability. An outside supplier might not be able to guarantee either, and any hold up in delivery might be serious. In any case there may be delivery charges to be added to the tender price and no information is available about how long the price of £1.00 is valid. Future price increases could be substantial. Should the tender have come from a foreign supplier there would be even greater uncertainties of delivery. It is also possible that import duties or quotas might be imposed, and future prices could also be adversely affected by exchange rate fluctuations.

The firm may have to lay off some workers if it accepts the tender. This could entail redundancy payments to those affected, and it might worsen industrial relations with the members of any trade union involved. It could well be better to continue manufacturing the component.

There is also the question of the fixed costs that the firm would incur. Would these merely be re-allocated, or is there a chance of avoiding them in the long run? Only in the latter case would there be long-run benefits. Finally, it would be wise to continue production only if no increase in variable costs is expected.

(b) It would be unwise to continue production of the component if weekly requirements may be expected to increase, because the firm's average variable costs increase at higher levels of output; the tender price then looks even more attractive. From this it may also be possible to use the firm's resources in other ways at greater profit. The firm should also consider the capital equipment used to produce the component. If its life is nearing its end, there will be added risks of interruption of production, and costs of repairs to be faced. This would make it wise to abandon production now, especially if replacement costs of equipment are high.

A further point is that the tenderer may be a specialist able to offer improved quality as well as a lower price. He may even allow extended credit terms with consequent benefit to the firm's cash flow. These are added reasons for ceasing production. The cost of production of the component should be expressed as a percentage of the total cost of the finished product. If this percentage figure is high it would be another reason for accepting the low tender price. It would be even more important to do this if it is thought that, in the price ranges concerned, the demand for the end product is price elastic. If that is the case it would be possible to make a marginal cut in selling price, if the component is bought in, and earn a higher total revenue.

QUESTION 4—AVERAGE TOTAL COSTS—SHORT-RUN COMPARISONS

The diagram below shows the short-run average total cost functions of three hypothetical companies, A, B and C.

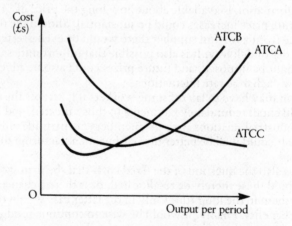

(a) What would you expect to be the characteristics of firms A and C?
(b) Which, of firms A and B, is the more efficient, and why?

[*January 1983, London*]

SUGGESTED ANSWER

(*a*) The diagram shows that the lowest average total cost of firm A occurs at a much lower level of output than is the case for firm C. The slope of the ATC curve of firm C is not so steep as that of the ATC curve of firm A, and it is likely that if the ATC curve of firm C were produced further it would show a flat-bottomed characteristic. It can, therefore, be assumed that firm C produces on a much larger scale than firm A.

The gentle slope of the ATC curve of firm C indicates that it has a relatively high element of fixed costs compared with its variable costs. It is, therefore, likely to be the more capital intensive of the two firms. On the assumption that the firms are in the same industry and that the market is oligopolistic, firm C is the likely market leader since it has the capacity to produce high levels of output at low average total costs. Because of these high levels of putput and low average total costs one may infer that firm C is likely to indulge in extensive advertising to sell its output. It is also likely that this firm carries out more extensive research and development programmes than firm A.

Firm A has, therefore, lower fixed costs, a smaller output capability and a desire for higher prices than does firm C.

(*b*) The efficiency of a firm is usually measured in Economics by reference to its lowest ATC. Taking this as the criterion, firm B is more efficient than firm A. An examination of the ATC curves of these two firms shows that up to the point at which these curves intersect firm B is the more efficient, but at higher levels of output firm A consistently achieves lower ATC values. The answer to the question asked thus depends on the definition of efficiency that is used and on the level of output chosen for comparative purposes.

5

Income Distribution and Organisation of Production

QUESTION 1—DIMINISHING RETURNS

You are given the following information:
Cost per tonne of fertiliser = £140
Fixed cost of land = £3,000
(Assume that no further costs are incurred.)
Selling price of wheat = £2 per unit.

Tonnes of fertiliser applied to a fixed area of land	Total production (units)
0	1,000
1	1,100
2	1,250
3	1,500
4	1,900
5	2,150
6	2,275
7	2,350
8	2,380
9	2,330

(a) With reference to the above data, comment on the relationship between the application of fertiliser and the production of wheat.
(b) What level of fertiliser would a profit maximising farmer choose to apply? Show the amount of wheat produced and the profit earned. Justify your answer.

[June, 1983, London]

SUGGESTED ANSWER

(a) The relationship between the application of fertiliser and the production of wheat illustrates the law of diminishing returns. The law states that as successive units of a variable factor (fertiliser) are added to a fixed factor (land), there will come a point where the

48

Calculations

Fertiliser (tonnes)	Total production	Change in total prod.	Change in average output	Marginal product	Marginal revenue (£)	Marginal cost (£)
0	1,000	—	—	—	—	—
1	1,100	100	100	100	200	140
2	1,250	250	125	150	300	140
3	1,500	500	166.66	250	500	140
4	1,900	900	225	400	800	140
5	2,150	1,150	250	250	500	140
6	2,275	1,275	212.5	125	250	140
7	2,350	1,350	192.8	75	150	140
8	2,380	1,380	172.5	30	60	140
9	2,330	1,330	147.77	−50	−100	140

increase in output (marginal product) falls. Eventually marginal product becomes negative which results in a fall in total output. Marginal product equals average output when the latter is at a maximum.

There are, therefore, three stages of diminishing returns:

1. Diminishing marginal returns occur after 4 tonnes of fertiliser have been applied. Any additional units of fertiliser add less to total production than preceding units. Total and average increases in output are still positive.
2. Diminishing average returns occur after 5 tonnes of fertiliser have been applied. Any additional units of fertiliser cause the average output to fall. Total output continues to increase but at a slower rate.
3. Negative marginal returns occur after 8 tonnes of fertiliser have been applied. Any additional units of fertiliser cause total output to decrease.

In the data given there was a more than proportionate increase in output from the application of 1 to 4 tonnes of fertiliser. This situation of increasing marginal returns was made possible by a more advantageous combination of factors of production. Initially, additional units of fertiliser allowed the land to be used more effectively. With a fifth tonne of fertiliser, however, the variable factor proved to be an imperfect substitute for the fixed factor, land. At this point diminishing returns set in.

(*b*) A profit maximising farmer would apply 7 tonnes of fertiliser. Up to this quantity the marginal revenue of each tonne (price × marginal product) exceeds the marginal cost (constant at £140 per tonne). Profit can, therefore, be increased with each successive tonne of fertiliser applied up to this point. Applying an eighth tonne would reduce profits by £80, which is the amount by which its marginal revenue falls short of the marginal cost.

The profit maximising quantity is 2,350 tonnes and total revenue is equal to this output multiplied by its price, i.e. 2,350 × £2 = £4,700. Total cost is equal to the fixed cost of land plus the variable cost of 7 tonnes of fertiliser, i.e. £3,000 + £980. Therefore, profit is equal to total revenue less total cost, i.e. £4,700 − £3,980 = £720.

QUESTION 2—REGIONAL POLICY

Gross domestic product per head of population
(United Kingdom = 100)

	1971	1975	1979
North	87.1	94.9	93.0
Yorkshire and Humberside	92.7	94.9	95.4
East Midlands	95.6	96.7	98.6
East Anglia	94.6	92.3	94.0
South East	113.8	112.8	113.4
South West	94.0	90.4	91.6
West Midlands	102.9	99.8	96.4
North West	96.3	96.2	95.9
Wales	88.0	89.9	88.4
Scotland	93.3	96.7	96.6
Northern Ireland	75.4	76.0	77.5

Source: *Regional Trends 1981*

(*a*) (i) Describe the regional variations in gross domestic product per head of population in 1979   (*3 marks*)
(ii) Suggest causes for the regional variations you have described
                                                                      (*4 marks*)
(*b*) To what extent was British regional policy successful in reducing regional disparity during the nineteen seventies?   (*5 marks*)
                                                        [*June 1983, A.E.B.*]

SUGGESTED ANSWER

(*a*) The data indicates considerable differences between regions in per capita income. In the South East it is substantially above the national average. In all other regions gross domestic product per head is below the UK average to a greater or lesser extent. Northern Ireland is prominent in showing much lower average income than the other regions. It is followed by Wales with the second lowest level of per capita GDP.

(b) The regional variations in GDP per head are partly due to regional disparities in unemployment rates. The South East with the highest per capita income also has the lowest rate of unemployment, since many of the newer industries have chosen locations near the principal markets. Conversely, areas such as Wales have suffered from structural unemployment. Extensive unemployment resulted from the working out of coal resources and the fall in demand for steel and other metals. Similarly, Northern Ireland figures reflect the decline in demand for ships, aircraft and textiles made from linen.

The location of economic activity affects the regional demand for labour. Differences in regional incomes can also be accounted for by differences in the supply of labour. For example, labour in the South East is likely to possess a higher level of education, and labour in the West Midlands a higher level of engineering skill, than their counterparts in other regions. This enables each unit of the workforce to make a greater contribution to output. Furthermore, there is a stronger tradition in the South East for married women to take paid work. Working wives may be less acceptable in some other regions, although it is impossible to separate this supply factor as a possible influence on GDP per head from the demand factor arising out of the shortage of employment opportunities.

Differences in occupational structures between regions are another explanation of differences in their average incomes. The demand for labour is derived from the final product which it helps to produce. London is a centre of finance and the demand for financial services is reflected in the salaries of people who provide them. Similarly, the relatively high GDP per head in Scotland, is a reflection of the earnings of the workforce involved in the extraction of North Sea oil.

The GDP of Northern Ireland has probably been adversely affected by civil disturbances during the decade.

(c) The pattern of regional disparity displays little change during the 1970s. The South East had the highest GDP per head in 1971 and was in the same position in 1979. Northern Ireland had the lowest GDP in 1971 and was also lowest in 1979. There has been some change of position for the regions in between, but not significantly.

Most regions with a GDP per head below average at the start of the decade had improved their relative position between 1971 and 1975. The North, for example, had an income per head of 12.9 per cent below the UK average in 1971, but only 5.1 per cent below the national average in 1975. After 1975, however, some of the assisted regions grew less rapidly than the UK as a whole, the relative position of the North had worsened so that its per capita income was 7 per cent

below the UK average by 1979. There had also been a reversal of
previous improvements by Wales.

Government attempts to divert economic activity from unassisted
to assisted areas appear to have been unsuccessful, and considerable
regional disparities remain. This does not mean that regional policy
has been without impact. It is impossible to assess what would have
been the relative position of development areas without government
assistance, but it is highly likely that the differences would have
widened.

Regional policy has been instrumental in attracting foreign and
domestic investment to assisted areas, without which their per capita
income would have been considerably lower. Northern Ireland, the
recipient of the greatest amount of regional aid, remained bottom of
the league. Nevertheless, the region's GDP per head moved closer to
the UK average in spite of civil unrest, and this can be viewed as a
measure of progress. Conversely, the West Midlands, which has not
received any assistance from regional policy, displayed the most
outstanding fall in relative GDP per head. Government intervention
has, therefore, been unable substantially to eliminate differences
between regions, but it has been successful in preventing these
differences from becoming more pronounced.

QUESTION 3—DISTRIBUTION OF INCOME AND WEALTH

Table 1   Distribution of income before and after tax in the United Kingdom

		1972/3		1977/8	
		Income before tax (percentages)	Income after tax (percentages)	Income before tax (percentages)	Income after tax (percentages)
Top	10%	26.9	23.6	26.1	23.4
Next	11–20%	15.8	15.8	16.3	16.2
Next	21–50%	33.3	33.9	33.5	34.0
Bottom	50%	24.0	26.7	24.1	26.4

(*a*) Distinguish between income and wealth   (*2 marks*)
(*b*) Describe the distribution of

    (i) income before tax in 1972/3 and 1977/8   (*2 marks*)
    (ii) marketable wealth in 1978   (*2 marks*)

Table 2 Distribution of wealth in the United Kingdom

	Marketable wealth (percentages)	1978 Marketable wealth plus occupational and state pension rights (percentages)
Most wealthy 1% of population	23	13
Next 2–5% of population	21	12
Next 6–10% of population	14	11
Next 11–25% of population	25	21
Next 26–50% of population	12	22
Bottom 50% of population	5	21

Source: *Social Trends*

(c) Account for the differences between

  (i) the distribution of income before and after tax in 1977/8
  (4 marks)

  (ii) the distribution of income before tax in 1977/8 and marketable wealth in 1978 *(4 marks)*

  (iii) the distribution of wealth before and after pension rights are included in the definition of wealth *(4 marks)*

  [June 1983, A. E. B.]

SUGGESTED ANSWER

(a) Income is a flow over a given period of time. It originates from the sale of factor services in the form of wages/salaries, interest, profit and rent. Wealth is the total stock of assets which exists at a given point in time and which have a money value. Personal wealth includes houses, company securities and bank accounts.

(b)(i) The differences in distribution of income before tax between 1972/3 and 1977/8 were marginal. In both cases over 26 per cent of pre-tax earnings accrued to 10 per cent of the population. This compares with 24 per cent of pre-tax earnings which accrued to 50 per cent of the population. The remaining 50 per cent share of income accrued to the other 40 per cent of the population. The most significant redistribution over the five-year period was within the top 20 per cent; there was a fall of 0.7 per cent of income accruing to the top 10 per cent and an increase of 0.5 per cent accruing to the next highest 10 per cent.
  (ii) The top 1 per cent of wealth holders owned 23 per cent of marketable assets while the bottom 50 per cent of wealth holders owned only 5 per cent of marketable assets. Taking the 10 per cent

most wealthy as a whole, they owned 58 per cent of marketable assets. Forty per cent of the population owned 37 per cent of marketable assets, leaving only 5 per cent of marketable wealth for the rest of the population. Put another way, the wealthiest 10 per cent of the population owned marketable assets in excess of that held by the other 90 per cent.

(*c*)(i) The difference in the distribution of income before and after tax in 1977/8 was slight. The top 10 per cent of earners had their share of income reduced by 2.7 per cent from 26.1 per cent to 23.4 per cent. The share of the 10 per cent just below the top strata fell by just 0.1 per cent. The next 30 per cent increased their share of income by 0.5 per cent, while the bottom 50 per cent of income recipients increased their share by 2.3 per cent.

The marginal contraction of differentials is a result of progressive income tax and transfer payments. Under a progressive system of taxation, a higher proportion of income is paid in tax as income rises (in 1977/8, the top rate of income tax was 83 per cent). Increasing marginal rates of tax will significantly reduce the disposable incomes of high earners compared with those of low earners. Progressive taxation, therefore, reduces post-tax income differentials. Transfer payments such as pensions and supplementary benefits represent income received without some productive service being given in return. They are used to redistribute income and increase the share accruing to low income recipients.

The extent of progression illustrated by the data is minor and this may be explained by the 'poverty trap'. Income is taxed at relatively low levels while entitlement to benefits is lost.

(ii) In 1977/8, the distribution of marketable wealth was far more unequal than the distribution of pre-tax incomes. The top 10 per cent owned 58 per cent of wealth compared with the top 10 per cent of earners who received 26.1 per cent of total income. Similarly the corresponding figures for the bottom 50 per cent were 5 per cent of wealth and 24.1 per cent of income.

The concentration of wealth is a reflection of lack of wealth tax in the UK and the ineffectiveness of Capital Transfer Tax. Capital Transfer Tax is considered by many accountants to be a 'voluntary' tax since it is relatively easy to avoid. Most of the wealth owned by the top 10 per cent is likely to have been inherited rather than accumulated out of earnings during the holder's lifetime.

In contrast, income tax is far more difficult to avoid and heavy taxation of income has resulted in payment through fringe benefits. A vast array of benefits is given to top salary earners and these benefits are often preferred to increments on highly taxed income. They include subsidised meals, free medical insurance and company cars.

These fringe benefits—many of which are not liable to tax—represent additions to real income. If they were to be included in calculations of income distribution, a far more skewed pattern would emerge.

(iii) The distribution of wealth after pension rights are included is far more equal than the distribution of marketable assets. Marketable wealth represents assets the ownership of which can be transferred. The largest single item is dwellings. Since nearly half the population live in rented accommodation, home ownership will have little relevance for the 5 per cent of marketable assets owned by the least wealthy 50 per cent of the population. Conversely, the value of dwellings will feature heavily among the wealth held by those at the apex of the wealth pyramid.

However, much of the country's wealth is in the form of pension rights. Their value can be measured either in terms of contributions already made or the capital and income they are expected to provide in the future. Every employee is compelled by law to participate in a state or occupational pension scheme. Many pension funds invest in marketable assets, particularly stocks and shares. Pension rights, therefore, represent indirect ownership of wealth, even though it cannot be marketed since the individual is unable to exchange pension rights for money. Pension rights are distributed more evenly throughout the population than marketable assets and help to disperse the ownership of wealth.

QUESTION 4—TRADE UNION MEMBERSHIP

Study the two tables which give information about trade union membership in the UK and then answer the questions which follow.

Table 1   TUC membership

Year	No. of Unions	Men (millions)	Women (Millions)	Total (Millions)	Percentage of total Men	Women
1955	183	6.7	1.3	8.1	84	16
1965	172	7.0	1.6	8.7	81	19
1970	150	7.2	2.1	9.4	77	23
1976	113	8.0	3.0	11.0	73	27
1978	112	8.5	3.4	11.9	71	29
1980	107	8.2	3.4	11.6	70.6	29.4

(Totals do not always match due to rounding).

(*a*) Account for the changes in TUC memberships disclosed in Table 1.   (*12 marks*)

Table 2   Growth of non-manual trade unions

Year	Non-manual workers in trade unions	Non-manual as percentage of total trade union membership
1965	1.8 million	18
1970	2.5 million	27
1973	2.9 million	31
1977	4.3 million	36

Source: *TUC Notes for Teachers*

(*b*) Account for the growth of non-manual trade unions disclosed in Table 2.   (*8 marks*)

SUGGESTED ANSWER

(*a*) The first change observed is the fall in the number of unions over the 25-year period during which 76 unions ceased to be members of the TUC. This is a fall of 41.5 per cent, a large change. At first sight it might be thought that this signifies a loss of interest in trade unionism, but total membership of unions was increasing for both sexes throughout the period. The changes in the number of unions must, therefore, have been the result either of amalgamations between unions, or the resignation from the TUC of certain unions. An example of the former was the amalgamation of the National Association of Schoolmasters with the Union of Women Teachers in order to comply with the change in the law on sex discrimination.

The second change observed is the steady increase in the number of members of trade unions up to 1978. This was due in part, to the increase in the workforce resulting from the post-war 'bulge' in the birth rate. This generation entered the workforce during the 1960s, and up to 1978 there was a period of relatively full employment. Recruitment was, therefore, facilitated particularly as workers saw the strength of collective bargaining in protecting their real wages as inflation increased. After 1978 the decline in male membership can be linked to the rapid increase in unemployment and early retirement which affected older industries such as mining, shipbuilding and steel manufacture where the work force is predominantly male.

The third change observed is the growth in the proportion of women members which has gone on steadily throughout the 25 years. This is linked to the increased participation of women in the workforce on a career basis. Family planning has enabled more women to limit births and so make it possible for them to pursue long-term careers. They therefore take seriously the benefits of trade union membership, particularly with regard to security of tenure and 'fair' pay. It is also true that since 1978, in several industries, more men than women have lost their jobs.

(b) The growth of non-manual trade unions reflects the structural changes which have been occurring in British industry since 1965. Unemployment has been greatest in older industries where craft unions once flourished, and more recently unskilled workers who might be members of general unions have also lost employment.

At the same time industries have arisen using or making new technology as, for instance, in electronics, microprocessors and word processors. The greatest advances in information technology probably came after 1977, but change was under way from 1970.

The manufacture of these new items can hardly be considered a manual task in the original sense of the term; instead it calls for scientific or technical skills.

The use of new technology is often associated with the growth of service industries in which professional skills are exercised. Many workers of these kinds have become more receptive to trade union ideals and have responded to the vigorous recruitment campaigns organised by the Association of Scientific, Technical and Managerial Staffs (ASTMS); the Local Government Officers' Association (NALGO): and the Association of Professional, Executive, Clerical and Computer Staff (APEX).

QUESTION 5—MANUFACTURING OUTPUT, EMPLOYMENT AND PRODUCTIVITY

Manufacturing output, employment and productivity: downturns and upswings

		Percentage changes in	
	Output	Employment	Output per man hour
1969–71	−0.7	−3.4	+2.9★ (+1.4% p.a.)
1971–73	+11.5	−2.8	+13.6 (+6.6% p.a.)
1973–75	−8.1	−4.2	−1.2 (−0.6% p.a.)
1975–78	+4.4	−3.2	+7.2 (+2.3% p.a.)
1978–81	−14.7	−15.6	+5.0 (+1.6% p.a.)
1981–83★★	+1.1	−9.4	+9.5 (+4.6% p.a.)

★1969–71 = output per person employed. ★★1983 average estimate.

Source: *Barclays Bank Review*, February 1984.

(a) Distinguish between output per person employed and output per man hour.   (4 marks)

(b) What is unusual about the relationship between output and productivity in 1981–3 compared with previous cycles?   (6 marks)

(c) Account for the increases in productivity in 1981–3.   (10 marks)

SUGGESTED ANSWER

(*a*) Output per person employed is the volume of output produced on average by each person in employment. Output per man hour is the volume of output produced on average in one hour by each person in employment. Output per head is adjusted to output per hour by taking overtime and short-time into account.

(*b*) The highest annual growth in productivity took place in 1971–3 and corresponded to a substantial growth in output of 4 per cent per annum. The more modest upswing of 1975–8 produced annual growth in productivity of 2.3 per cent which was marginally above norm and corresponded to a growth in output of 1.5 per cent per annum. Conversely the downturns of 1969–71, 1973–5 and 1978–81 are associated with small or negative increases in productivity. This pattern contrasts sharply with the relationship between changes in output and productivity between 1981–3. Negligible growth in output of 0.5 per cent a year corresponds to a substantial improvement in productivity of 4.6 per cent per annum. Against the background of what had occurred in previous cycles, the rapid increase in productivity is unusual because it is not accompanied by any significant growth in output to facilitate the absorption of under-utilised capacity.

(*c*) The 1981–3 improvements in productivity reflect a number of factors such as the installation of new capital investment and reductions in restrictive labour practices which allowed existing capital to be used more efficiently. However, the data indicates that increases in productivity have also been achieved by large contractions in employment at a time when output showed a marginal increase. The 4.6 per cent annual increase in productivity was accompanied by a reduction in employment of nearly 5 per cent a year. This rate of unemployment was slightly exceeded in 1978–81 but this was to be expected in a period of downturn when output also fell considerably.

There are two ways in which higher unemployment may bring about higher productivity. Firstly, in a period of severe recession, the least efficient marginal firms with low productivity are forced to cease production. Consequently there is a move from low productive employment to zero employment. This raises the average for those workers who remain in employment. The question raised is whether improved productivity can be sustained in the long term when demand increases. Less efficient firms may resume production and, as a result, productivity will deteriorate.

Secondly, output per head is increased by demanning among firms which continue to produce. The reductions in overmanning during the 1973–5 downturn were limited because firms had expectations,

based on past experience, of an imminent upswing in economic
activity and did not want to incur costs of firing and rehiring.

An unusually deep and prolonged recession has led to more
pessimistic expectations. The anticipated upswing did not materialise
and the intensity of the subsequent financial squeeze was reflected in
the shedding of labour earlier and faster. In the past, much of this
labour would have been carried, and the 1981–3 contraction in
employment is partly a lagged response to the oil price rises of the
1970s and the decreases in demand associated with previous cycles.
When firms ceased to hoard labour, productivity improved. In this
case, reversal of productivity gains is less likely during a period of
economic recovery.

QUESTION 6—PRODUCTIVITY OF CAPITAL

Output per unit of capital:
Manufacturing, 1980

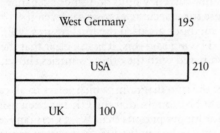

Increase in output per increment
in capital: Manufacturing

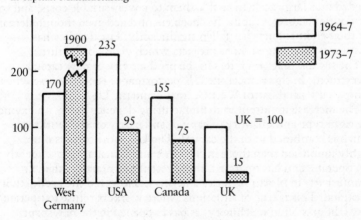

Source: *Economic Progress Report*, May 1984

Study the two charts relating to output per unit of capital in manufacturing industry, and then:

(*a*) Discuss the probable reasons for the relatively poor performance of the UK.   (*10 marks*)
(*b*) Discuss possible methods of improving output per unit of capital in manufacturing.   (*10 marks*)

SUGGESTED ANSWER

(*a*) In the first place it must be pointed out that diagrams of this sort do not always state precise and exact relationships. One reason for this is that, because capital items depreciate and depreciation is highly subjective, all valuations of capital goods are likely to be subject to margins of error. Values will also depend on the method of depreciation used. Furthermore, national valuations in one currency must be converted into other currency units and since exchange rates fluctuate there is room here for inaccuracies to arise. Even if purchasing power parity methods are used the final figures will, at least, be approximations. Having said this, it is still clear that the UK has performed poorly compared with the other countries shown in the diagrams.

Considering the first of the two diagrams which refers to all capital, irrespective of age, it might be thought that the UK has been using older capital equipment for longer periods than West Germany and the USA. This would mean a failure in the UK to invest in capital with a higher marginal productivity. In fact this has occurred in shipbulding and steel making. In these industries, subsidies have been needed on a large scale to enable them to cover variable costs, and so the continued use of capital has been encouraged even though demand for their end products has fallen significantly. Fiscal policy has, therefore, encouraged those projects which yield poor returns.

The second diagram refers to the productivity of new capital investment. In this respect the UK performance is even worse when compared with those of West Germany and the USA.

The increase in output in manufacturing depends partly on having the right type and quantity of capital, and partly on the workforce which is combined with the capital. The UK workforce is more highly unionised than those in the USA and Canada. Consequently it can operate, and has operated, more restrictive practices than its counterparts in North America and this has lowered the productivity of capital. This is true of situations where workers refuse to operate new labour-saving machinery, as has happened in the newspaper industry and the Post Office.

In the UK there is a proliferation of trade unions based on particular crafts or skills. West Germany is in marked contrast as it has a much smaller number of unions most of which represent all the workers in a particular industry. The large number of unions in the UK has been a disadvantage, which has led to inter-union disputes over job demarcations, and to leap-frogging wage claims aimed at preserving wage differentials. Management in the UK has generally been inferior to that in West Germany and Japan where managers have been able to command more loyalty and dedication from their workforces. The end result of all this has been a poor level and standard of output in the UK coupled with rising wage costs. Dearer and inferior goods have lost markets, and left manufacturers with the need to reduce output. Hence, much new capital is under-utilised in the UK.

(*b*) UK experience shows that it is necessary to reach a better understanding with the work force about the introduction of new forms of capital. This may necessitate a new approach to retraining, redundancy and early retirement. Owners of businesses undertake investment in new capital if they believe that the marginal cost of the capital will be less than its marginal revenue product. Incentives to invest would be greater if interest rates were reduced and the opportunity to make profits was better. It would, therefore, help if Corporation Tax were reduced so that owners would benefit more from new investment. A further way of providing this benefit in the short run would be to allow shorter periods of time for writing off, as depreciation, the cost of new capital items. In the very long run, government could revise policy so that subsidies were withdrawn from declining industries. This would stop investment in capital items used to make goods for which there was a permanent decline in demand.

A more positive step would be to follow monetary and fiscal policies aimed at increasing the effective demand for manufactured goods. This might enable manufacturers to run capital equipment at a higher level of capacity and so increase output per unit of capital.

6

Trade

QUESTION 1—INCOME ELASTICITY OF DEMAND FOR UK IMPORTS AND EXPORTS

Comment on the significance for the British economy of the figures shown below and on the difficulties in interpreting them.

Industries with a money income elasticity of demand for imports greater than 2, and export elasticities of the same commodities, 1963–74.

	UK income elasticity of demand for imports	World income elasticity of demand for UK exports
Motor vehicles	3.7	0.9
Linoleum, leather cloth, etc.	3.5	1.2
Men's and boys' tailored outerwear	3.2	1.7
Radio and other electronic apparatus	2.9	1.8
Cans and metal boxes	2.8	0.6
Motor cycles	2.7	0.9
Plastics moulding and fabricating	2.6	1.7
Domestic electrical appliances	2.6	1.1
Insulated wires and cables	2.6	1.0
Iron castings, etc.	2.6	1.3
Furniture and upholstery	2.5	2.2
Tobacco	2.5	1.1
Bedding, etc.	2.4	0.6
Overalls and men's shirts, underwear, etc.	2.4	2.0
Other textile industries	2.4	1.1
Pharmaceutical and toilet preparations	2.3	1.4
Women's and girls' tailored outerwear	2.3	1.1
Weatherproof outerwear	2.3	0.7
Miscellaneous manufacturing industries	2.3	1.8
Metal industries not elsewhere specified	2.2	1.2
Cardboard boxes, etc.	2.2	1.3
Dresses, lingerie, infants' wear, etc.	2.2	1.3

	UK income elasticity of demand for imports	World income elasticity of demand for UK exports
Telegraph and telephone apparatus	2.2	1.0
Production of man-made fibres	2.1	1.3
Other drink industries	2.1	1.0
Glass	2.1	1.2
Wire and wire manufactures	2.1	0.9
Miscellaneous stationers goods	2.1	1.1
Biscuits	2.1	1.3
Other electrical goods	2.1	1.3

(Source: A P Thirwall, *National Westminster Quarterly Bank Review*, February 1978)

[*June 1980, London*]

SUGGESTED ANSWER

For every category listed, domestic income elasticity of demand for imports is greater than the corresponding world income elasticity of demand for UK exports. During a world recession, this position concerning relative income elasticities can be advantageous to the UK balance of payments. As world incomes contract, UK demand for imports will fall at a faster rate than world demand for UK exports. This has been partly responsible for the recent improvement in the UK non-oil balance. When the UK was experiencing negative growth rates, demand for the imports listed fell by a proportionately greater amount. This also applied to some UK exports as the incomes of other countries contracted, but always to a lesser extent. For some exports, such as bedding and motor cycles, the decrease in demand was proportionately less than the fall in world income.

In contrast, relatively high income elasticity of demand for imports has adverse implications for the UK balance of payments during a period of recovery. The figures indicate that the level of UK imports will rise at a faster rate than her exports as world incomes increase. To take the example of motor vehicles, a 10 per cent increase in UK income will lead to a 37 per cent increase in demand for imported vehicles. This compares unfavourably with a 9 per cent increase in world demand for UK vehicles if other countries' incomes increase at the same rate. Consequently, balance of payments problems are likely to impose a constraint on UK growth compared with international competitors. Without revenue from North Sea oil, the visible balance will worsen progressively as world recovery gets under way. Furthermore, imports of manufactured goods are substitutes for home production. If imports rise faster than exports, the growth in UK national income will be hampered. A slow rate of growth will, in turn, limit investment and employment opportunities.

The policy implications of the data are that the UK should employ revenue from North Sea oil to develop industries which can produce goods for which there is a high world income elasticity of demand. The production of quality manufactured goods using advanced technology is a possible field of profitable expansion.

There are a number of difficulties in interpreting the data because it is incomplete. The table concentrates on manufactured goods and even in this area of production, there are omissions. The lack of information concerning these omissions, primary goods and invisible items prevents a full analysis.

Similarly, the product groups for which data is given are quite wide and averages may disguise important differences between individual goods within the same category. For example, the income elasticity of demand for family saloons is likely to differ from the income elasticity of demand for commercial vehicles. World income elasticity of demand is also an average which may disguise significant differences between countries, and not all countries are of equal importance in British export trade. Another difficulty concerning averages is the time span of 11 years. Since data is not given for individual years, it is important to know if there have been any changes in trend. It is also difficult to assess the significance of the data for the balance of payments because no information is given relating to the proportion to total import expenditure and export revenue represented by each category.

Another difficulty of interpretation arises if changes in growth rates display a difference in direction or magnitude between countries. It is highly unlikely that all countries will experience simultaneously the same rate of increase or decrease in their national incomes. Interpretation of the data would have to be revised to take any differences into account.

Finally, there is the assumption that a change in the level of income is the only variable involved. Changes in other factors such as the distribution of income and international trade barriers will also have an important bearing on interpretation. Movements in the terms of trade are particularly important. These may occur partly as a result of differences in domestic inflation rates and partly as a result of alterations in exchange rates. If the UK visible balance deteriorates during a period of world recovery, sterling is likely to depreciate. In other words, import prices rise and export prices fall to counteract the effect of an increase in world incomes. This makes price elasticity of demand for imports as relevant as income elasticity, and compounds the difficulties in interpreting the data.

QUESTION 2—IMPORT COSTS AND EFFECTS OF EXCHANGE RATE CHANGES

A UK importer of microcomputers operating in a competitive market quotes the following prices to dealers.

	Quantity purchased in a month			
	Less than 5	5–19	20–39	40 and over
Price per unit (£)	1625	1575	1525	1450

An additional rebate of £25 per machine is given provided that (i) orders are placed in batches of ten or more and (ii) payment is made immediately on despatch of the machines.

The above prices are based upon an exchange rate of $ (US) 2.30/£1. Any fall in the price of sterling might cause surcharges to be applied to the above prices.

(*a*) Assuming the above prices reflect the importer's costs, what can be inferred about these costs from the above information?
(*b*) In which circumstances would you advise this importer to pass on a fall in the price of sterling to his dealers?   [*January 1984, London*]

SUGGESTED ANSWER

(*a*) The most heavily discounted unit price is £1,425 which is equivalent to $3,277.50 at the given exchange rate. The importer must, therefore, be able to purchase each machine at less than these figures. The lowest selling price represents a discount of just over 12 per cent on the highest selling price and from this it can be inferred that: (a) the importer achieves significant cost savings when executing bulk orders, and (b) that a prompt addition to his cash flow avoids the necessity to pay relatively high interest rates on overdrafts. The cost savings on bulk orders are most likely to arise from economies in the use of delivery vehicles and economies in invoicing. Further administrative costs are avoided when cash is paid immediately on despatch of goods since there is no need to send reminders to debtors, no risk of bad debts arising, and no need to keep personal ledger accounts.

It is, however, the dollar cost of a microcomputer which is the most significant of the importer's costs. Should the price of sterling fall to $2.00/£1 then to maintain profit margins the most heavily discounted price would have to be £1,638.75 which is an increase of over £213.

(*b*) The first thing to be considered is the price elasticity of demand for the product. If this has a value less than unity a sterling price rise is most likely to be passed on to a dealer, because when demand is price inelastic an increased price does not have a markedly adverse effect on revenues.

A second point for consideration is whether the change in the exchange rate is expected to be long-lasting or not. If a system of fixed exchange rates existed there would be a much stronger case for passing on the fall in the price of sterling than if exchange rates were freely floating. In the latter case, if sufficient stocks had already been purchased it might be possible to defer further imports to see how the exchange rate would perform in the near future.

The importer would also need to consider the position of other suppliers of microcomputers. They may be selling machines the prices of which are not initially denominated in dollars. Assuming that these machines are considered by consumers to be acceptable substitutes for those mentioned in the question it would only pay for our UK importer to raise his prices if these competitive machines also increased in cost.

QUESTION 3—UK CURRENT ACCOUNT BALANCE 1970–82

With reference to the diagram 'Current Account Balance of Payments 1970–82'

(*a*) Give examples of the main items which make a positive contribution to UK invisible earnings.   (*3 marks*)
(*b*) Assess the contribution of invisible earnings to the UK balance of payments in this period.   (*9 marks*)
(*c*) Account for the changes in the UK visible balance between 1970 and 1982.   (*8 marks*)

SUGGESTED ANSWER

(*a*) Invisibles comprise those international transactions in which no tangible item is directly involved. The main items which make a positive contribution to UK invisible earnings fall into two broad categories: (a) services, particularly sea transport, civil aviation, tourism, banking and insurance; and (b) interest, profits and dividends which are the returns of British investment overseas.

(*b*) The trade in invisibles has been consistently in surplus, ranging between £0.8 billion in 1970 to £3.4 billion in 1976. These surpluses have made a significant contribution to the UK balance of payments. For most of the period 1970–82 the invisible surplus was about £2 billion, and it was of paramount importance in helping to alleviate the

Current Account Balance of Payments 1970–82

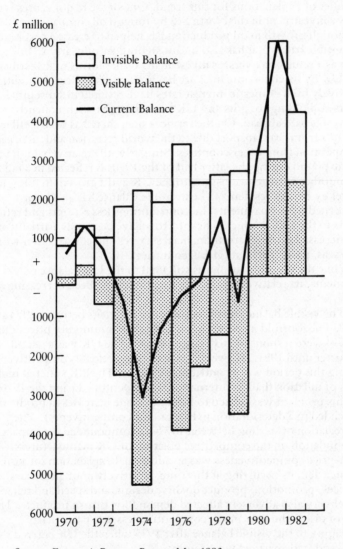

Source: *Economic Progress Report*, May 1983

deficits on the visible balance which occurred, with the exception of 1971, throughout the 1970s.

The overall surplus on the invisible balance has, however, declined in relative importance both as a proportion of world trade and as a proportion of the UK's current balance. The decline in relative importance of invisibles is most evident in 1980–2. There are a number of explanations for this trend. One of the major causes is the heavy investment in the North Sea by foreign oil companies. Although growth in oil production has helped to create a surplus on the visible balance, it has also meant an outflow of nearly £3 billion a year as a return on overseas investment. Other forms of investment in the UK by foreign companies are having a similar effect. In addition, relatively high domestic interest rates have resulted in substantial overseas holdings of gilts and UK bank deposits. Consequently interest is paid abroad. On the services side, there has been a fall in receipts from sea transport due to the world recession and increasing competition from other countries. Similarly, the relatively high value of the pound during the latter half of the 1970s is reflected in a fall in the number of overseas visitors to the UK and a growth in foreign travel by British residents. The invisible balance has also been weakened by net payments, i.e contributions less receipts and refunds, made to the EEC budget. These factors have been only partially offset by increased earnings from financial services and construction work overseas, particularly in OPEC countries.

While the invisible surplus is still vital to the UK balance of payments, its relative importance has, therefore, been decreasing.

(c) The visible balance displays substantial deficits between 1973 and 1979. The fourfold increases in oil and other commodity prices during 1973–4 were responsible to a large extent. (The UK was a net oil importer until 1981.) However, lack of international competitiveness during this period was a contributory factor. The UK suffered higher rates of inflation than its international competitors during the 1970s.

This problem was related to below average increases in productivity which led to a deterioration in labour cost competitiveness. The appreciation of sterling between 1977–81 compounded the impact of high inflation on the competitive position of UK manufacturers. Non-price competitiveness was an additional explanation for visible balance deficits occurring at this time. Relatively poor after-sales services, promotion, product quality, design, and speed and reliability of delivery also adversely affected demand for British products. The lack of price, and non-price, competitiveness was particularly damaging to the visible balance after 1973 when the UK entered the EEC and trade barriers were removed.

The UK had become almost self-sufficient in oil during 1980, but the visible balance surplus in that year was largely a result of the British economy experiencing earlier and deeper recession than the rest of the world. This led to a large fall in imports during the second half of 1980. A further increase in the visible surplus in 1981 was due to the continuing rise in overseas sales of oil; the UK had become a net exporter of oil by this time. Non-oil visible trade returned to deficit in 1982, but the growing surplus on oil, assisted by a large oil price increase in 1979, kept the visible balance in surplus.

Although the success on the visible balance is overwhelmingly a result of oil production, increased competitiveness has been a contributory factor since 1981. This has been achieved by a fall in the external value of the pound, increases in productivity and reductions in cost and price inflation to levels which are more in line with overseas competitors.

QUESTION 4—EEC BUDGET CONTRIBUTIONS

The European Community Budget 1981

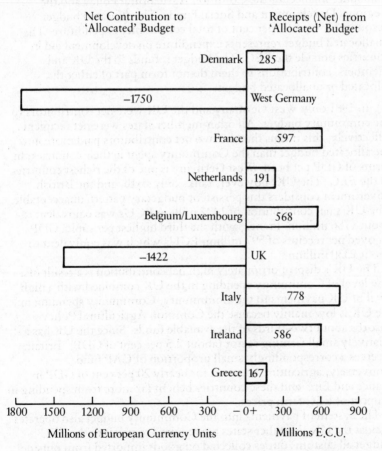

Net Contribution to 'Allocated' Budget		Receipts (Net) from 'Allocated' Budget
	Denmark	285
−1750	West Germany	
	France	597
	Netherlands	191
	Belgium/Luxembourg	568
−1422	UK	
	Italy	778
	Ireland	586
	Greece	167

1800 1500 1200 900 600 300 − 0+ 300 600 900

Millions of European Currency Units   Millions E.C.U.

Source: *Economic Progress Report Supplement*, October 1982

(*a*) Distinguish between the 'allocated' and 'unallocated' budget
(*4 marks*)
(*b*) Examine the causes of the high UK net contribution to the
Community budget.   (*10 marks*)
(*c*) Suggest *three* measures for reforming the system of budget
contributions and receipts.   (*6 marks*)

SUGGESTED ANSWER

(*a*) The allocated budget represents expenditure within the EEC.
It includes finance for the Common Agricultural Policy and the
Regional Development and Social Funds. The allocated budget
accounts for over 90 per cent of total community expenditure. The
unallocated budget represents expenditure on development aid in
countries outside the EEC. The budget refunds to the UK and
members' contributions to them do not form part of either the
allocated or unallocated budget.

(*b*) In 1981 only West Germany and the UK were net contributors to
the community budget. All other member states were net recipients.
Effectively, this means that the two net contributors paid more into
the allocated budget than the Community spent in their countries. In
terms of GDP per head, West Germany is one of the richest countries
in the EEC. The UK, however, ranks only sixth, and the British
government considers this persistent budgetary pattern unacceptable.
The UK's net contribution of 1422 million ECUs was equivalent to
about £786 million. France, with the third highest per capita GDP
enjoyed net receipts of 597 million ECUs which was equivalent to
about £330 million.
 The UK's disproportionately high net contribution is a result of a
low level of Community spending in the UK combined with a high
level of UK payments to the Community. Community spending in
the UK is low mainly because the Common Agricultural Policy
absorbs about two-thirds of the available funds. Since the UK has a
relatively small farming sector (about 2.5 per cent of GDP), Britain
receives a correspondingly small proportion of CAP funds.
Conversely, agriculture accounts for nearly 20 per cent of GDP in
France and Eire, and these countries benefit far more from spending in
support of EEC farm prices.
 The system of payments into the Community budget also operates
against the UK. Member states are required to pay into the EEC
budget all customs duties collected on goods imported from outside
the Community, agricultural import levies (the difference between

EEC prices and world prices) and up to 1 per cent of VAT. A larger than average proportion of the UK's trade is still with countries outside the Community. As a result, the UK collects for the EEC comparatively large sums in customs duties and agricultural levies. (These payments are likely to decline in the future as UK trade with the rest of the EEC increases.) Britain is also penalised by the VAT system. As one of the poorest countries in the Community, the UK has a high propensity to consume. Since most consumption is subject to VAT a relatively high proportion of GDP is collected in indirect taxes and up to 1 per cent passes to the Community.

(c) The problem of the UK's high net contributions, which is unrelated to her ability to pay, has been acknowledged by other EEC members. In the four years between 1980–83, the UK received budget refunds of over £2,500 million, constituting about two-thirds of the unadjusted net contributions. These refunds have had to be negotiated annually and a number of reforms have been suggested as a means to a permanent solution.

First, EEC expenditure could be restructured so that the regional and social funds are allocated a greater proportion of the total, especially in relation to CAP finance. This will facilitate increased spending on Britain's depressed regions.

Second, the VAT levy contributions could be replaced by payments based on per capita GDP. In this way, relatively prosperous countries would bear the heaviest budgetary burdens.

Third, agricultural spending could be restrained by limiting the range of products eligible for support or by setting production ceilings beyond which guaranteed prices will be cut. Such limits have already been applied to cereal and dairy production, but such measures are likely to prove unpopular with Eire and France.

QUESTION 5—INTERNATIONAL TRADE

Study the graph below showing changes in the shares of world trade in manufactured goods, and answer the following questions:

(a) Account for the changes which occurred in the decade 1945–55.
(7 *marks*)

(b) Account for the changes which occurred in the period 1955–75
(7 *marks*)

(c) Account for the changes which occurred after 1975 and suggest possible economic consequences if these trends continue through the 1980s. (6 *marks*)

Shares of the world trade in manufactured goods

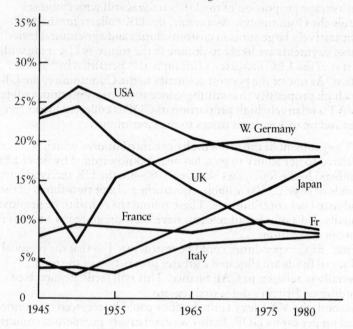

(Source: *Barclays Bank Review*)

SUGGESTED ANSWER

(a) The decade 1945–55 was the immediate post-war period following the Second World War. Of the countries dealt with in the diagram only two had escaped severe damage to their capital assets and manufacturing capability—the USA and the UK. The worst damage had been suffered by West Germany. Until 1950 the USA, which had sustained no damage by war to its factories, had every chance to export manufactures on a world-wide basis. The USA was also contributing through the Marshall Aid scheme to the restoration of the war damaged economies of victors and vanquished alike. France and the UK, each with its colonial connections and dependencies, were both anxious to resume their pre-war trade with these areas, and needed to earn foreign currency to pay off loans made by the USA. These two European powers often restricted the sale of manufactures at home in order to meet foreign demand. Hence the upswing of UK and French exports until 1950. In these same five years West Germany was too preoccupied with domestic reconstruction to divert many of its goods to export markets, and had, in any case, lost access to its former colonies.

In the last five years of the decade Japan made headway in export manufactures mainly because of its marked labour cost advantages. West Germany began to reap the benefit of vast investment in modern buildings, machinery, plant and equipment. It also had the benefit of a dedicated labour force organised into relatively few trade unions. The UK, on the other hand, experienced more labour disputes and its industries suffered on occasions from inadequate fuel supplies. Its cotton industry began to lose markets to Japanese producers. Italy, at this time, was slower than other countries to modernise and rationalise its industries.

(*b*) The years 1955–75 saw the Japanese make large inroads into markets previously the preserve of the UK and the USA particularly in textiles at first, but followed later by motor-cycles, cars, ships, televisions and electronics. The Japanese continued to enjoy such significant cost and productivity advantages that not only did they invade successfully the overseas markets of the UK and USA, but even the domestic markets of those two countries.

A second matter of great importance was the emergence of the EEC and the subsequent lowering, and eventual removal, of restrictions on the trade in manufactures between the member countries. Of importance, too, was the common external tariff against non-members which emerged. These events combined in favour of West German and Italian exports and to the detriment of the USA and the UK. Even when the UK joined the EEC it still lost in the world market because of its lack of competitiveness and poor reputation for delivery on time. Despite this the UK made considerable progress in non-manufacturing activities. What is noteworthy is the failure of France to increase its share of world trade in manufactures. This was due partly to loss of colonial markets as colonies gained independence and partly to a failure to control costs at competitive levels. West Germany and Italy, on the other hand, were able to make significant improvements in their shares of the market in motor vehicles. It is also relevant to note that considerable quantities of American production were being absorbed by the Vietnam war, the space programme and greater domestic consumption.

(*c*) From 1974/75 to the present day production and world trade have been adversely affected first by the large oil price rises and then by the general recession resulting from, among other things, higher energy costs. For all of the countries shown on the chart there have, therefore, been only marginal changes in market share during this period with the exception of Japan. Her continued increase in share of the world trade in manufactured goods is a reflection of her continued cost advantages (despite heavy dependence on expensive imported oil) and her ability to change from the less profitable lines (e.g. shipbuilding) to more profitable lines (e.g. video recorders). Japan has also increased her penetration of the UK market in motor vehicles. Up to 1980, the UK continued to lose ground due to high unit labour costs and falling demand for the products of old industries like shipbuilding.

A continuation of these trends through the 1980s is likely to lead to a growth of protectionism in the USA and the UK by way of quotas and/or import duties in order to protect jobs and the balance of payments. Such measures would slow economic growth in Japan and encourage Japanese producers to try to avoid these controls by setting up production in the USA and UK. Examples can already be seen in the case of BL and Nissan in the UK and the desire of Toyota to get a base in the USA. Should barriers to Japanese exports not be put up it is likely that standards of living in Japan will rise at the expense of those in the UK and France where unemployment will be more difficult to resolve. The UK may thus be forced even more to base her economy on services, because any benefits to employment and the balance of payments from North Sea oil are likely to be relatively short-lived. Other countries shown on the graph look likely to experience only slow rates of economic growth, even if they hold their market shares.

QUESTION 6—THE MOTOR CAR INDUSTRY

Study the following data about the car industry and then answer the questions which follow:

UK new car registrations

	1980	% of market	1979	% of market
Ford (UK)	247,946	16.38	248,550	14.48
Ford imports	216,760	14.3	237,009	13.8
Total Ford	464,706	30.7	488,559	28.29
BL (UK)	259,075	17.1	320,233	18.66
BL (Belgium)	16,723	1.1	16,723	0.97
Total BL	275,798	18.22	336,984	19.63
Vauxhall (UK)	82,233	5.43	94,731	5.52
Vauxhall imports	26,985	1.78	17,667	1.0
Total Vauxhall	109,218	7.2	112,398	6.5
Talbot (UK)	62,876	4.15	83,072	4.8
Talbot imports	27,998	1.8	36,361	2.1
Total Talbot	90,874	6.0	119,433	6.95
Total imports	858,319	56.70	965,910	56.28
Total market	1,513,761	100.00	1,716,275	100.00

(*a*) What was the percentage decline in the total market from 1979 to 1980? (*2 marks*)

(*b*) When all four major domestic producers were faced with a declining market suggest reasons why they continued to import cars from their factories outside the UK. (*10 marks*)

(*c*) In view of the relatively poor showing of BL suggest reasons why the government continues to support it whilst refusing support to Talbot. (*8 marks*)

SUGGESTED ANSWER

(*a*) Between 1979 and 1980 car sales fell from 1,716,275 to 1,513,761—a fall of 202,514 units. As a percentage of 1979 sales this is

$$\frac{202,514 \times 100}{1,716,275 \times 1} = 11.8 \text{ per cent}$$

(*b*) In view of the declining market for cars, the factories outside the UK must have had some significant advantages to the multi-national companies which own them, otherwise demand for cars in the UK would have been met from domestic sources. The factories outside the UK are located mainly in France, Belgium, West Germany and Spain. With the exception of West Germany each of these countries has cheaper labour than the UK. In all of them labour relations are better than in the UK, so productivity per man year is better, and so average costs of production are advantageous. These costs were further reduced in most cases by government assistance to the car industry outside the UK and the low rates of inflation abroad. In 1979 and 1980 the pound was relatively strong against other European currencies and so it was possible to sell in the UK cars which had been produced abroad, at relatively low prices whilst making satisfactory profits.

The operation of a number of different plants enables car manufacturers to rationalise production of their various models, concentrating on one or two types in each locality. In this way, the greatest internal economies of scale can be achieved with further benefits to cost and, hence profits. Thus, whilst certain models would be imported by the UK on a large scale, others could be exported.

As multi-national companies, the car makers regard their market as the entire world. They are, therefore, in a position to indulge in pricing policies and manufacturing policies which take advantage of favourable tax treatment by governments; so it may well pay to operate in a number of countries. There is also the fact that having production units in different locations safeguards supplies of cars especially at times of local labour disputes. Car manufacturers have invested much capital abroad and it is very expensive to transfer these investments to new locations.

(*c*) Of firms listed in the question, BL is the only one wholly owned in Britain. In 1979/80 the main shareholder was the British government which had committed very large sums of tax-payers' money to major investment projects being undertaken by this manufacturer. This testified to the government's belief in the future potential of BL.

BL was the direct employer of a very large workforce. Indirectly, it gave employment to many workers engaged by other firms making car components. BL also exports a large volume of products and so is very important to the UK balance of payments. Were BL to go out of production, the UK market would be even more open to foreign firms—with consequent damage to the UK balances of trade and payments.

Talbot is a foreign-owned company with a smaller domestic production than BL and the smallest share of the total market (6 per cent) in 1980. Compared with the market shares in 1979 both BL and Talbot had lost ground, but Talbot's loss was relatively the greater and BL still had three times as much of the market as Talbot. In view of these facts and the fact that the smallest number of imports came from BL (Belgium) it is not surprising that BL (UK) should continue to enjoy the support of the government.

7

Money and Banking

QUESTION 1—MONEY SUPPLY

The government aims to reduce the rate of monetary growth as an integral part of its economic strategy. No single measurement of the money supply, such as M3, can serve as an adequate monetary indicator. Monetary targets are set for both broad and narrow definitions of money stock. Monetary growth in excess of the targets set will limit the possibility of tax cuts which are favoured by some politicians.

1. Explain why different definitions of the money supply are thought necessary. *(12 marks)*
2. Define M3. *(2 marks)*
3. Under what economic conditions are politicians likely to advocate tax cuts? *(6 marks)*

SUGGESTED ANSWER

(*a*) Money serves as a medium of exchange. There is, however, no clear-cut distinction between money (available for making purchases) and long-term deposits (which are not). This difficulty makes necessary a number of different definitions of the money supply. Each measurement of the money stock is distinguished by its 'liquidity', i.e. the speed with which it can be used to make purchases. The broader the definition, the less sensitive it is to differences in interest rates. On the other hand, a broad definition of the money supply is more difficult to measure quickly and to control.

M0, M1, M2, £M3 (Sterling M3), M3, PSL1 and PSL2 (Private Sector Liquidity) constitute the measurements of the money supply (in order of liquidity, starting with the most liquid) currently used by the UK authorities. Although the government has chosen Sterling M3 as its main official target, different definitions are considered necessary because it is by no means certain which measure (if any) is most closely linked to the inflation rate.

It is also necessary to gauge the extent of 'disintermediation' which is the process whereby bank customers make use of savings and credit facilities outside the banking system. Disintermediation may arise because of government control of bank credit and/or changes in interest rate differentials. To concentrate solely on Sterling M3 is misleading because bank deposits (included in £M3) may be converted, for example, into building society deposits (which do not form part of £M3). The wider measurement PSL2 remains unaffected by this kind of switch because it incorporates both bank and building society deposits.

Finally there is a tendency for any officially controlled measurement of the money supply quickly to lose its significance. During 1979 and 1980 the tight controls on bank credit through the application of the corset (Supplementary Special Deposits) led to an expansion of PSL at the expense of Sterling M3. When the corset was removed, it soon emerged that evasion of the corset controls had taken place on a massive scale. When the corset regulations limited bank credit, commercial bills were used to provide finance for firms in need of money. (Commercial bills form part of PSL but not £M3.) Conversely, lifting the corset regulations greatly increased Sterling M3 relative to PSL. Hence, different definitions are necessary to facilitate government policy aimed at a sustained reduction in the rate of growth of every measurement of the money supply.

(*b*) M3 is composed of notes and coins in circulation plus all bank deposits, whether denoted in sterling or foreign currencies, held by British residents.

(*c*) All other things being equal, tax cuts will result in an expansion of the money supply and aggregate demand. A tax cut not matched by reductions in public expenditure will increase the PSBR. If this is financed by government borrowing from banks, a faster rate of monetary growth will ensue. Such a policy may be viewed as appropriate when the economy is operating at below full capacity and experiencing relatively low levels of employment, investment and economic growth.

These problems can be alleviated by application of the multiplier and accelerator principles; they depend upon increased consumption which can be achieved through tax reductions. A weakened balance of payments position and a higher inflation rate are, however, possible repercussions which may become manifest after a time lag of approximately eighteen months. Consequently a cabinet is most likely to favour tax cuts as a general election approaches. This policy is often subsequently reversed in order to avert a sterling crisis.

QUESTION 2—EFFECTS OF INFLATION

Given below are some price indices for three years.

	1968	1973	1978
Retail prices	100	143	302
of which:			
Food	100	158	358
Input prices (basic materials and fuel)	100	158	389
Average price of new dwellings (on mortgage)	100	231	381
Import prices	100	150	357
Export prices	100	138	335
Terms of trade	100	92	94
Average weekly earnings of males in manufacturing industry	100	176	359

(Source: *The British Economy in Figures*, Lloyds Bank Ltd 1979)

(a) 'These indices clearly show that the average adult male in manufacturing industry has gained during a period of inflation and, therefore, inflation is in the general interest.' Discuss.

(b) Evaluate, in the light of these figures, the effect of inflation on house buyers.

[*June 1981, London*]

SUGGESTED ANSWER

(a) Throughout the 10-year period, the earnings of the average adult male increased at a faster rate than the index of retail prices. The assumption that inflation is in the general interest does not, however, necessarily follow. A problem arises because the relevance of statistical averages used to support the proposition is questionable. Individual patterns of expenditure may not conform to those employed in the construction of the retail price index. Those with large families, for example, may spend a larger than average proportion of their income on housing and this has increased in price at a faster rate than the cost of living generally. The low paid are also unlikely to reflect the consumption patterns assumed by the retail price index since a larger proportion of their income tends to be spent on essentials. The indices for food, fuel and house prices were consistently higher than the general index. Consequently the rise in the cost of living for low income groups would have been correspondingly greater than the average.

A further difficulty arising out of the use of statistical averages is that the change in income for the average adult male in manufacturing may not have been typical of the workforce as a whole. He is most likely to benefit from trade union bargaining strength which can often ensure that earnings keep pace with inflation. Non-union labour (female employees in particular), those who work outside the manufacturing sector and people reliant on fixed incomes may have suffered a loss in real income during this period. The unemployed and others dependent on welfare benefits are in a similar position; increases in transfer payments usually lag behind price rises.

From a monetarist standpoint, unemployment is a function of inflation. The loss of international competitiveness results in fewer jobs in the domestic economy. During the first 5-year period, import prices rose at a faster rate than export prices, and this is indicated by a worsening of the terms of trade. The rise in import prices, however, is largely a reflection of increases in the price of oil and other commodities for which the UK has a relatively low price elasticity of demand. Conversely there exists a high price elasticity of demand for UK exports. The situation in the period 1973–78 was even less satisfactory.

Import prices rose by 138 per cent while export prices rose by 143 per cent. Rising costs and prices force up the price of UK exports. If inflation in competitor countries is at a lower rate, the demand for UK goods, both at home and abroad, will fall and a rise in unemployment will ensue in the long term. At the same time, the balance of payments position will deteriorate and lead to a depreciation in the external value of sterling. This will, in turn, lead to higher imported input costs which cause inflation to accelerate.

The economy is further weakened by the effects of inflation on savings and investment. While the erosion in the value of savings is partially offset by rising nominal interest rates, the high cost of borrowing acts as a disincentive to invest. Ultimately this results in a lower level of economic growth and employment.

In conclusion, rising prices can be distressing for a significant proportion of the population which suffers a fall in real income while other sectors enjoy increased standards of living. Equally important are the long-term effects in terms of low levels of investment and economic growth, balance of payments deficits and increased unemployment. Inflation cannot, therefore, be said to be in the general interest.

(*b*) In the first 5-year period, the price of new dwellings rose by 131 per cent while the average earnings of males in manufacturing rose by 76 per cent. In the second 5-year period, the figures were 65 per cent and 104 per cent respectively. Taking the 10-year period as a whole, a 381 per cent rise in the price of new dwellings compares with a 359 per cent increase in average earnings. The effect of this depends on whether the house buyer is a potential purchaser or already in the process of buying a home before the changes take place. The position of the potential purchaser has worsened. Maximum mortgages allowed by building societies, banks and insurance companies are calculated as a multiple of the borrower's annual earnings. The gap between this figure and the price of dwellings has widened. This means that in some cases, the mortgage applicant will not be able to borrow sufficient funds to make a purchase unless a larger deposit is available. In other cases the prospective buyer will be forced to purchase a smaller or lower quality dwelling.

Additional problems arise because costs associated with house buying are often related to the price of the dwelling. Conveyancing fees and stamp duty will, for example, have shown corresponding increases. To buy a house in 1973, therefore, required a substantially higher level of savings relative to income when compared with the same purchase in 1968. These problems had eased by 1978, since earnings had increased at a faster rate than house prices during the period 1973–78.

The difficulties facing prospective purchasers did not affect existing buyers unless they wanted to move to a more expensive property. Assuming they remained in their existing homes, buyers would have benefited from a substantial capital gain (although usually unrealised) which more than compensated for the higher mortgage interest charges associated with periods of inflation. Exemption from taxation is allowed if a house buyer decides to realise the capital gain on the owner's only, or main, dwelling.

QUESTION 3—FINANCE FOR INDUSTRY

'The failure of UK industry to invest in new plant in the 1970s was said to be a major contribution to the country's poor economic performance. The funds were available from banks but competition for these funds was fierce. Banks are in the business of making money, and they lend to the sector which is most lucrative, and this raises the cost of borrowing in other sectors. Lending to private individuals is generally more lucrative and safer, so in consequence there are insufficient investment funds for the company sector.

Other countries do not face the same consequences of the relative attractiveness of private lending. Their governments provide funds for the banking institutions to lend to companies for long periods. This leads to greater lending to the company sector and to a better economic performance both with respect to economic growth and the Balance of Payments.

These facts point to a need to turn economic orthodoxy on its head

in the UK and abandon demand manipulation in favour of supply
management.'

(Adapted from *The Guardian*, 24 October 1979.)

Referring to the above quotations, answer the following:

(*a*) Discuss whether the government economic policy outlined above
really 'turns economic orthodoxy on its head'.
(*b*) 'Subsidising one form of lending and not another will always lead
to a distortion of the market for capital.' Discuss.

[*June 1982, London*]

SUGGESTED ANSWER

(*a*) Economic orthodoxy may be thought of as allowing market forces
to prevail in markets so that the price mechanism brings supply and
demand to equilibrium.

The capital market in the UK is not perfect. There are relatively few
lending institutions and there are certain very large and influential
borrowers such as the government itself and the multinational
companies. There is also a lack of perfect knowledge about market
conditions among the participants in it. So far as demand for loanable
funds is concerned, economic orthodoxy would indicate that
corporate borrowers respond only to the price of such funds.
However, that is not the only consideration. Political certainty and the
estimated M.R.P. of capital are just as important. Economic
orthodoxy is, therefore, already to some extent 'turned on its head'.

It is true that banks have traditionally been most interested in
relatively short-term lending at market rates of interest, subject to
there being adequate security available for the loan. They have,
however, recently been willing to lend to the corporate sector for
longer periods and have charged different borrowers different rates of
interest. It is not, however, always true that private individuals always
get preference over corporate borrowers; they often present greater
risks and offer inferior security than corporate bodies. In the UK
demand manipulation has been a significant part of government policy
since Keynes advocated it, but this also involves some stimulus to the
market mechanism. Governments have, however, also pursued
policies of supply management. Examples concerning the supply of
loans may be found in the open market operations and calls for special
deposits by the Bank of England, as well as its use of funding of
government debt. These techniques can increase or decrease the ability
of banks to lend according to the way in which the techniques are
used. If this results in good use of such funds economic orthodoxy has
not been 'turned on its head'.

The passage quoted in the question seems to assume that the greater availability of capital to the corporate sector will, *per se*, produce better economic growth and improve the balance of payments. Such a view is over-optimistic since there is no guarantee that corporate bodies will use funds economically or efficiently. Loans provided by governments through banking institutions reduce the risk for banks which may, therefore, be less strenuous in their examination of the risks involved and returns expected. These loans may merely provide the means for the short-term survival of firms in permanent decline and in these cases economic orthodoxy has been 'turned on its head'. There is no guarantee that funds borrowed will be used to buy domestically produced capital goods. On the other hand, if funds are tight at home, capital can be raised abroad. In each of the two latter cases the balance of payments may be adversely affected.

(*b*) The statement is largely true of the use of subsidies in any market, not only the market for capital. One reason for this is that it is difficult to ensure that capital made available at a subsidised rate is, in fact, used for the purpose for which it was initially provided. Examples of this are well known in the UK economy where in the early 1970s there was considerable speculation in real estate. Here, money lent at favourable rates ostensibly for productive purposes was diverted to speculative uses. There was also the practice of 'round-tripping' where bank interest rates had been held below market levels because that was government policy. This allowed borrowers to have access to relatively cheap credit which could then be on lent at higher rates to other borrowers not so favoured by the banks. The market for capital was thus distorted by the emergence of a dual rate of interest; and this would be likely to recur if the government subsidised loans for specific purposes. To avoid this situation would require the use of other forms of control on the use of borrowed funds. These controls would add to the administrative costs of government and would be difficult to enforce effectively. Their very existence would further distort the market for capital. Funds made available at subsidised prices will result in abnormally high demand for them and, being cheap, may be put to uses which would not be considered worth while in a free market; so distortions will occur. In the UK funds offered for house purchase are, in effect, subsidised so far as the private purchaser is concerned by virtue of income tax relief on mortgage interest payments, and by the long repayment periods allowed. The effect of this has been to bring about a much larger proportion of home owners in the UK than in other countries where such favourable treatment does not exist.

Footnote   Candidates should note the date of the newspaper article—October 1979. Subsequent to its publication the economic policy of the UK government has turned towards supply management in the field of loan capital. Three schemes of this sort are worthy of note.

(*a*) *The Business Start Up Scheme*   This was begun in 1981 for a three-year term and gave 'outside' investors tax relief at their top marginal rate on investments up to £20,000 in selected new businesses.

(*b*) *The Loan Guarantee Scheme*   This also started in 1981 for three years and in it the government provided £150m per year. This sum acted as a guarantee for up to 80 per cent of loans to applicants who had no previous acceptable business experience or were unable to provide adequate security from their personal resources.

(*c*) *The Venture Capital Scheme*   This was introduced in 1980 and allows losses on equities in some unquoted companies to be offset against income tax liability.

Answers which showed awareness of one or more of these schemes would probably have been awarded the highest marks.

8

Employment and National Income

QUESTION 1—THE MULTIPLIER IN REVERSE

Recorded below are some figures for a hypothetical economy.

		Weeks			
		1	2	3	4 ...n
1	Output (=income)	100	90	82	75.6...50
2	Investment	10	10	10	10 ...10
3	Consumption goods produced (=consumption goods demanded in previous week)	90	80	72	65.6...40
4	Planned (ex-ante) savings (=20% of row 1)	20	18	16.4	15.1...10
5	Consumption goods demanded (=80% of row 1)	80	72	65.6	60.5...40
6	Excess supply (=row 3 minus row 5)	10	8	6.4	5.1... 0
7	Planned savings minus planned investment (=row 4 minus row 2)	10	8	6.4	5.1... 0

(Source: W. Beckerman, *An Introduction to National Income Analysis*, Weidenfeld & Nicolson, 1968.)

(*a*) Specify and briefly explain the process which is at work over time in the case of the above economy.
(*b*) The last column on the right shows the values of the variables for a national income equilibrium.
 (i) What assumptions are necessary for this equilibrium to be reached?
(ii) When will the equilibrium be reached?

[*June 1981, London*]

SUGGESTED ANSWER

(*a*) The process at work is the national income multiplier in reverse. A rise in the desire to save causes a considerably greater fall in the level of national income. With reference to the data, the sequence of events occurs as follows:

1   In the original relationship savings and investment constitute 10 per cent of national income.
2   In week 1, households decide they would like to save 20 per cent of income while the level of investment remains the same.
3   Consequently, firms find themselves with unsold goods since consumption goods demanded is now 80 and consumption goods produced is 90. (In week 1 unsold goods = 10)
4   In week 2, firms reduce output, and therefore income, so that production of consumer goods is equal to the 80 demanded in the previous week. (Row 3)
5   Households, however, save 20 per cent of the new reduced income leaving the demand for consumption goods at 72. (Row 5 of week 2)
6   In week 3, firms reduce output still further in order to eliminate excess supply over demand (8 in week 2).
7   The sequence continues until income falls to 50. At this level of income savings generated are equal to 10 which in turn is equal to the level of investment and equilibrium is restored.

(b)(i)   There are a number of assumptions implicit in the data. First, investment is assumed to be an autonomous expenditure, i.e. while it affects the level of income, it is unaffected by it. Second, savings are assumed to be a function of income and the marginal prosperity to save is constant at 20 per cent. In reality the marginal propensity to save is likely to decline with a fall in income. Third, the model assumes that savings and investment are the only leakage and injection operating. This implies a closed economy with no government activity. Imports, exports, taxation and government expenditure would normally be expected to have an important bearing on the level of national income.

(ii)   Equilibrium will be reached when injections equal leakages or, in the model given, when planned savings, are equated to planned investment. At this level of output, there is no pressure on national income either to expand or contract.

QUESTION 2—GDP—EXPENDITURE COMPONENTS

1   What is meant by the terms: consumers' expenditure, government consumption, fixed investment, stockbuilding, adjustment to factor cost, GDP after factor cost adjustment, 1975 prices.
2   Calculate:
(a)   Total final expenditure for 1982
(b)   GDP at market prices for 1980

Expenditure components of GDP
(£ billion, 1975 prices—quarterly averages)

	Consumers' expenditure	Government consumption	Fixed investment	Stock-building	Total domestic demand	Exports	Imports	GDP*
1979	17.9	6.0	5.3	?	29.6	8.2	8.8	25.9
1980	17.9	6.1	5.1	−0.4	28.7	8.3	8.5	25.4
1981	18.0	6.1	4.7	−0.5	28.2	8.1	8.5	24.8
1982	18.2	6.2	4.8	−0.2	29.0	8.1	8.9	25.1
1982 Q4	18.5	6.2	4.9	−0.4	29.2	8.2	?	25.5
% changes								
1982 Q4 on 1979 H1	3½	4½	−5½	0.9†	−1	2	1	−1
1982 Q4 on 1981 Q2	3	2½	5½	0.3†	4½	2½	5½	3½

*After factor cost adjustment.
†Change in stockbuilding as a percentage of GDP.

(Source: *Economic Progress Report*, May 1983)

(*c*) Stockbuilding in 1979
(*d*) Imports in Quarter 4 1982, assuming net adjustment to factor cost = −£3.2b.
3   Briefly analyse the movements shown in the table.

SUGGESTED ANSWER

1   *Consumers' expenditure* represents expenditure on goods and services which are required by private consumers for the direct satisfaction of their wants. It includes spending on items such as food, entertainment and insurance services. Expenditure on consumer durables—videos, for example—also falls into this category.

Government consumption also represents day-to-day spending on goods and services, but by the public sector. It would include, for example, expenditure on furniture, stationery and heating for government offices. Transfer payments, such as welfare benefits, are excluded since they would give rise to double counting.

Fixed investment is expenditure on capital goods. That is, goods which are not required for direct satisfaction of wants, but because they provide the means for producing goods and services. It includes expenditure on items such as plant, machinery, road and hospitals. The gross figure does not make an allowance for replacement of capital. The net national product is calculated by subtracting capital consumption or depreciation from GNP.

Stockbuilding represents the value of physical increase in stocks and work in progress. Increases in inventories and semi-manufactured goods are assumed to have been purchased by the producer and added to other forms of expenditure in national income accounts. If the value of physical stocks and work in progress has decreased it is subtracted from the total because it does not represent current production.

Adjustment to factor cost. Expenditure is calculated at market prices, i.e. in terms of the prices at which products are sold. It includes, therefore, all expenditure taxes, such as VAT and excise duties, and excludes subsidies. To convert market prices to factor cost, expenditure taxes must be subtracted and subsidies added.

Gross domestic product after factor cost adjustment represents the value of all goods and services created by the factors of production in the national economy. It measures, therefore, the value of production in terms of the factor incomes generated. Imports are part of the production of other countries and do not generate income domestically. Consequently, they must be subtracted from total domestic expenditure to calculate GDP at factor cost.

1975 prices. Expenditure is initially calculated at prices which were current in the year spending took place. This makes comparisons with other years difficult because inflation would have resulted in an increase in money national income which does not necessarily correspond to any increase in output of goods and services. Consequently, current prices are deflated and national income measured in terms of prices applicable in a chosen base year. In this case prices are scaled down to 1975 levels. This enables changes in real, as opposed to money, national income to be measured.

2 (*a*) Total final expenditure = total domestic demand + exports

In 1982, total final expenditure = £29.0 + £8.1 (billion) = £37.1 billion

(*b*) GDP at market prices = total domestic demand + exports − imports

In 1980, GDP at market prices = £28.7 + £8.3 − £8.5 (billion) = £28.5 billion

(*c*) Stockbuilding = total domestic demand — consumers' expenditure — government consumption — fixed investment

In 1979 stockbuilding = £29.6 − £17.9 − £6.0 − £5.3 (billion) = £0.4 billion

(*d*) Imports = total domestic demand + exports − GDP at market prices

In 1982 Quarter 4 imports = £29.2 + £8.2 − £(25.5 + 3.2) (billion) = £37.4 − £28.7 (billion) = £8.7 billion

3   The *Economic Progress Report* stated that the table 'shows movements in the main expenditure components of GDP. Much of the continued recovery in total domestic demand during 1982 reflected the 3 per cent growth in consumer spending. During 1982 the savings ratio fell to around 10–11 per cent, helped by lower interest rates and lower inflation. The profile of real personal disposable income remained relatively flat before recovering a little in the fourth quarter to a level slightly below that in the first half of 1979, the previous cyclical peak. Total fixed investment increased by around 3½ per cent between 1981 and 1982, with rising investment in construction, distribution and services more than offsetting a continued fall in manufacturing. Renewed destocking in the third quarter of 1982 ran on into the fourth quarter—partly because distributors initially

responded to the upturn in consumers' spending by running down stocks. At the end of 1982 manufacturers' stocks remained rather high in relation to sales, while distributors' stocks in relation to sales were at their lowest level for six years'.

QUESTION 3—UNEMPLOYMENT AND UNFILLED VACANCIES

Great Britain: unemployment and vacancies, 1970–79
(Three months moving average, seasonally adjusted)

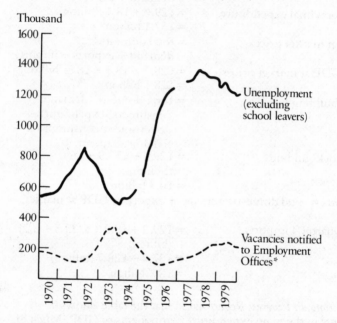

*Vacancies at Employment Offices are only about one third of total vacancies

(Because of industrial action, figures are not available for the periods November 1974 to March 1975 and November 1976 to March 1977. Figures for the period September to November 1974 include some estimates.)

(Source: Manpower Services Commission, *Manpower Review*, HMSO 1980)

(a) Explain briefly the meaning of 'seasonally adjusted' and its significance for the above figures.
(b) Discuss reasons why the figures for 'Vacancies notified' and 'Unemployed' tend to converge in some years and diverge in others.

[*June 1982, London*]

SUGGESTED ANSWER

(a) In some occupations the amount of employment available is dependent on changes in demand from one season of the year to another, or on changes in weather conditions associated with the different seasons. In assessing the long-term trends in statistics about employment and unemployment it is desirable to eliminate these seasonal factors, which might otherwise produce misleading figures. It must be realised that the figures of unemployment would have appeared higher but for the elimination of those who were out of work temporarily because of the seasonal nature of their work. One such example is the case of building and construction workers who tend to inflate the unemployment figures during periods of bad weather in the winter. Another example is that of the rise in unemployment figures associated with the large numbers of school leavers at the end of the summer term. Likewise, the vacancies notified statistics understate the actual number of vacancies for similar reasons. The net result of these adjustments is to reveal more clearly the long-term influences on employment.

(b) The first reason for the convergence/divergence of these figures is that they reflect the cyclical nature of recession and recovery. In 1971, and again in 1977, the UK economy was in a depressed state. Consequently, there were many unemployed and comparatively few vacancies which would have necessitated help to fill from Employment Offices. In a recession employers can often recruit labour from those who take the trouble to visit employers and ask about a job. On the other hand, in 1974, the UK economy was very active, so that it was consequently easier to find jobs and more difficult to find suitably qualified labour. Hence, more vacancies would have been notified to Employment Offices.

Over the 10-year period to which the statistics refer, changes were taking place in the size and composition of the working population of the UK. Both in 1971/72 and 1978/79 the working population increased as more school leavers appeared; so it is not surprising that there should have been at least temporary difficulties in absorbing these extra workers.

During this decade changes were occurring in methods of production which, in many cases, tended to become more capital intensive. This was partly due to inventions and improvements of capital equipment, and partly due to the rising costs of labour (especially after 1972).

To the extent that capital was substituted for labour one could expect higher levels of unemployment and lower levels of notified vacancies. The whole structure of the UK economy was undergoing radical change in the 1970s. Old industries such as shipbuilding and steel were in significant decline and, consequently, shedding labour in large amounts. The newly emerging industries such as electronics were much less labour intensive. This, again, added to unemployment.

Other changes were also taking place. For instance during the decade 1970–79 the employment situation worsened progressively with the result that many people did not register for work although they would have been prepared to take a job. Married women and people taking early retirement are examples in this category. Change was also taking place in the replacement ratio (social security payments as a percentage of wages net of tax). Before 1971 this was 76 per cent; currently it is less than 70 per cent. The third change occurred in the level of real wages demanded which generally tended to increase. The oil price rise in 1973 lowered the real income available to British workers, and this reduced the level of demand for labour at each real wage. This helps to explain the divergence after 1973.

Footnote: In June 1983 the base for the calculation of statistics for unemployment was altered so as to exclude: (*a*) Males over 60 years of age, and (*b*) Those out of work but not claiming social security benefit for unemployment (e.g. some married women and/or part-time workers).

QUESTION 4—THE PHILLIPS CURVE

(*a*) Explain and interpret the diagram below.

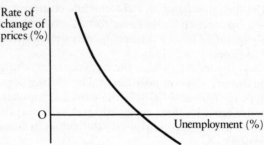

(*b*) In the light of the following figures, comment on the Phillips curve and the British experience during the period 1971–76.

Year	Rate of change of Retail Price Index (%)	Unemployment (%)
1971	9.5	3.4
1972	6.8	3.7

Year	Rate of change of Retail Price Index (%)	Unemployment (%)
1973	8.3	2.6
1974	15.9	2.6
1975	24.2	4.0
1976	15.7	5.4

[June 1983, London]

SUGGESTED ANSWER

(*a*) The diagram representing the Phillips curve, illustrates an inverse relationship between unemployment and inflation; increased unemployment resulting in less inflation and vice versa. In other words, there is a 'trade-off' between the two and the Phillips curve can be used to measure the opportunity cost of reducing inflation in terms of unemployment.

The Phillips curve implies that there is a level of unemployment, U, at which prices will be stable. Any increase in unemployment causes prices to fall. Conversely, any reduction in the unemployment rate will cause prices to rise. Moreover, the curve is non-linear. Successive reductions in the level of unemployment will cause progressively higher increases in the rate of price inflation. For example, if unemployment falls from U_1 to U_2, the rate of price inflation increases from P_1 to P_2. An equal reduction in the unemployment rate from U_2 to U_3 results in a much higher rate of price inflation from P_2 to P_3. As unemployment approaches zero, hyperinflation is likely to result.

The level of unemployment is an indication of the level of capacity utilisation within the economy. In short, the nearer the economy is to operating at full capacity, the higher the rate of inflation.

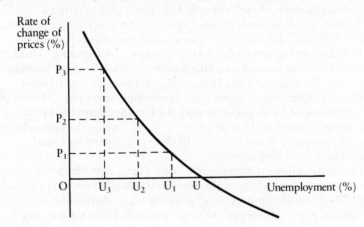

While the Phillips curve plotted a stable statistical relationship between the rates of inflation and unemployment, it did not, in itself, provide any causal explanations. The curve has, however, been interpreted as evidence of support for both demand-pull and cost-push theories of inflation. From a demand-pull perspective, low levels of unemployment are seen as an indication of 'bottlenecks' and excess demand for labour. As competing firms bid for scarce labour, wage rates will rise and this is reflected in a rapidly rising price level. From a cost-push perspective, low levels of unemployment are an indication of strong bargaining power among trade unions. Consequently, they are able to demand and obtain higher wages; these extra costs are then passed on to consumers in the form of higher prices.

(b) During the early 1960s an unemployment rate of $2\frac{1}{2}$ per cent was considered sufficient to ensure that inflation did not exceed around 2 per cent. The figures for 1971–73 indicate that the Phillips curve has shifted to the right. That is, higher rates of inflation correspond to a given rate of employment. The statistics for 1973–76 imply that the Phillips curve relationship may have broken down altogether. In 1973–74, the inflation rate increased independently of the unemployment position. In 1974–76, there was a direct relationship between unemployment and inflation rates, a situation known as 'slumpflation' or 'stagflation'. Hence, both the position and the shape of the Phillips curve are brought into question by the figures.

There are a number of factors which may have caused the Phillips curve to shift to the right. First, devaluation of sterling in 1967 and further falls in the external value of the pound after 1972 when exchange rates ceased to be fixed. This led to a rise in import prices which ultimately filtered through to domestic prices causing compensatory wage demands. Given the bargaining power of trade unions at this time, these demands were often met, creating a cost-price spiral. Second, another substantial rise in costs of imported inputs followed the increase in oil and other commodity prices in 1974. This had the same effect as the devaluation of sterling. Third, deflationary budgets reduced take-home pay while welfare benefits increased. This meant a rise in the replacement ratio, i.e. transfer payment entitlement expressed as a percentage of net pay. The rise in the replacement ratio, together with the introduction of redundancy payments, has reduced the incentive to work, in that the unemployed can take longer to find a new job. In short, voluntary frictional unemployment has increased.

Economists from the monetarist school deny that a trade-off between inflation and unemployment exists at all in the long run, and the 1973–76 figures appear to support this view. According to Friedman, expectations play an important role in the inflationary process. Trade unions lodge pay claims in an attempt to obtain real wage increases. They take into account not only current rates of inflation, but also price increases expected to occur in the future. Firms will attempt to recoup increased labour costs through increased prices, giving rise to a wage–price spiral. As a result, the Phillips curve is continuously shifting outwards. Moreover, it becomes unstable as inflation accelerates. Ultimately, the loss of international competitiveness among domestic firms causes bankruptcies and unemployment. Monetarists argue that this problem can only be solved when expectations of future inflation rates have been revised downwards. This requires tight control of the money supply and further increases in short-run unemployment during the process of adjustment.

QUESTION 5—NATIONAL INCOME EQUILIBRIUM

An economy at present has a national income = £80,000 million. The following relationships occur:

C	= 0.8Y DISPOSABLE.
Income tax	= 0.5Y
Indirect tax	= 0.1Y (there are no subsidies).
Imports	= 0.2Y.
Planned investment	= £12,000 million.
Government spending	= £60,000 million.
Exports	= £18,000 million.

For consumption, taxation and imports the average and marginal propensities are equal.

(a) Explain, in terms of injections and withdrawals, why the economy is not at present in equilibrium. (6)
(b) What is the equilibrium income? (4)
(c) The government wishes to achieve balance of payments equilibrium. What change in its own spending will enable this to be achieved? Explain briefly the process of change which is occurring. (10)

In any calculations show your working clearly.
[*June 1983, Southern Universities Joint Board*]

SUGGESTED ANSWER

CALCULATIONS

Disposable income = Income − Income tax
$$= Y - 0.5Y$$
$$= 0.5Y$$

Savings   = Disposable income − Consumption
$$= 0.5Y - (0.8 \times 0.5Y)$$
$$= 0.5Y - 0.4Y$$
$$= 0.1Y$$

Withdrawals   = Savings + Taxation + Imports
$$= 0.1Y + (0.5Y + 0.1Y) + 0.2Y$$
$$= 0.9Y$$

Injections   = Investment + Government spending + Exports
$$= £12,000m + £60,000m + £18,000m$$
$$= £90,000m$$

(a) Injections are additions to the circular flow of income that do not arise out of the spending of domestic firms on local factor services or the spending of domestic households on locally produced goods and services. There are three types of injections: investment, government spending and exports. They constitute injections of aggregate demand and cause the circular flow of income to expand. Withdrawals are leakages from the circular flow of income. That is, a withdrawal is any income which is not passed on through the purchase of domestic factor services or domestically produced goods and services. There are three types of withdrawals: savings, taxation and imports. They constitute leakages of demand and cause the circular flow of income to contract. For national income to be in equilibrium, withdrawals must equal injections. Under these circumstances the circular flow of income remains stable.

The economy represented by the data is not in equilibrium because injections are greater than withdrawals. Injections = £90,000 million. Withdrawals = 0.9Y

$$= 0.9 \times £80,000m$$
$$= £72,000 \text{ million}$$

(b) Since injections are greater than withdrawals, national income will expand. Withdrawals are a function of income and the process will continue until sufficient withdrawals have been generated to equal the current level of injections at £90,000 million.

Withdrawals   = 0.9Y

Therefore Equilibrium income $= \dfrac{£90,000m}{0.9}$

$$= £100,000 \text{ million}$$

(c) For balance of payments equilibrium to be achieved, imports must be equal to exports. That is, imports should equal £18,000 million. Since the propensity to import is constant at 0.2Y, balance of payments equilibrium is attained when

$$0.2Y = £18,000m \text{ and } Y = \frac{£18,000m}{0.2} = £90,000 \text{ million}$$

Withdrawals = Injections = 0.9Y
$$= 0.9 \times £90,000m$$
$$= £81,000 \text{ million}$$

Level of government spending
required = £81,000m − Investment − Exports
$$= £81,000m − £12,000m − £18,000m$$
$$= £51,000m.$$

Hence the government must reduce its own spending by £9,000 million from its current level of £60,000 million.

The process of change occurring is the multiplier in reverse. A decrease in injections achieved by government spending cuts of £9,000m causes national income to contract until withdrawals have fallen to the same level. At each stage of the multiplier process, the reduction in government expenditure will mean less income passed on in the circular flow which, in turn, results in less consumption and a contraction of withdrawals. The ripple effect continues until the level of national income is £90,000 million.

QUESTION 6—NATIONAL INCOME CALCULATIONS

(*a*) Use the following figures to calculate the national income by both the expenditure and income methods.

	£ billion (1980)
Value of physical decrease in stocks	3.6
Exports of goods and services	63.2
Gross trading profits of companies	24.9
Gross fixed investment	40.1
Income from employment	137.1
Capital consumption	27.0
Rent	13.2
Imports of goods and services	57.8
General government final consumption	48.3
Gross trading surplus of general government enterprise	0.2
Consumers' expenditure	135.4
Gross trading surplus of public corporations	6.0
Income from self-employment	18.4
Taxes on expenditure	37.3
Net property income from abroad	1.5
Stock appreciation	6.5
Subsidies	5.2
Residual error	0.2

(*10 marks*)

(b) Explain briefly whether the following should be included in calculating the national income:

   (i) A 40-year-old house originally costing £1,000 was resold for £50,000.
  (ii) The rent which could be obtained from an owner-occupied house and is estimated to be £5,000 a year.
 (iii) The amount paid in unemployment benefit if it increases by £100,000.
  (iv) A private employment agency makes £60,000 profit.
   (v) A pools syndicate wins £750,000.

(10 marks)

SUGGESTED ANSWER

(a)(i) *The Expenditure Method*

	£ billion
Value of physical decrease in stocks	−3.6
Exports of goods and services	63.2
Gross fixed investment	40.1
Imports of goods and services	−57.8
General government final consumption	48.3
Consumers' expenditure	135.4
Taxes on expenditure	−37.3
Subsidies	5.2
Gross domestic product at factor cost	193.5
Net property income from abroad	+1.5
Capital consumption	−27.0
National income	168.0

(ii) *The Income Method*

	£ billion
Gross trading profits of companies	24.9
Income from employment	137.1
Rent	13.2
Gross trading surplus of general government enterprises	0.2
Gross trading surplus of public corporations	6.0
Income from self-employment	18.4
Stock appreciation	−6.5
Residual error	0.2
Gross domestic product at factor cost	193.5
Net property income from abroad	+1.5
Capital consumption	−27.0
National income	168.0

(*b*)(i) The resale value of a 40-year-old house would not be included because it does not form part of production in the year in question.

(ii) Imputed rent is included. To exclude this item would mean that national income would fall as an increasing proportion of the population becomes home owners. This would give a false impression of changes in living standards.

(iii) Unemployment benefit is a transfer payment in that no productive service is given in return and is excluded from calculations. If the £100,000 increase in benefit was included, it would be double counting.

(iv) The £60,000 profits of the private employment agency are included. They represent payment for a productive service.

(v) A £750,000 pools win is excluded from the calculations because it constitutes a transfer of money from the majority of punters to the syndicate without any production taking place.

QUESTION 7—THE ACCELERATOR

Year	Demand (£s)	Capital required (£s)	Capital depreciation (£s)	Net investment (£s)	Gross investment (£s)
1	15,000	45,000	3,000	—	3,000
2	18,000	54,000	3,000	9,000	12,000
3	20,000	60,000	3,000	6,000	9,000
4	21,000	63,000	3,000	3,000	6,000
5	21,500	64,500	3,000	1,500	4,500
6	21,500	64,500	3,000	—	3,000
7	21,500	64,500	3,000	—	3,000
8	20,000	60,000	3,000	—	—

(*a*) Calculate the accelerator coefficient.
(*b*) Use the data to explain why the capital goods industry is subject to much greater swings in demand than the consumer goods industry.
(*c*) What assumptions are necessary for the accelerator process to take effect?

SUGGESTED ANSWER

(*a*) The level of new investment will be some multiple greater than the change in consumption. This multiple is called the accelerator coefficient and depends on the ratio of the value of capital equipment to the annual value of its output. $a = I_n/\Delta C$, where a = accelerator coefficient, I_n = net investment and ΔC = the change in consumption. In the example given, each £1,000 increase in consumption induces an increase of £3,000 in capital stock. The accelerator coefficient is, therefore, 3.

(*b*) Between year 1 and year 2, consumer demand increases by 20 per cent from £15,000 to £18,000. In order to accommodate the rise in consumption, there is a 400 per cent increase in investment from £3,000 to £12,000. In year 3, consumer demand continues to rise from £18,000 to £20,000. This is a slower rate of growth than the preceding year and leads to a fall in investment from £12,000 to £9,000. It is therefore the rate of change in consumption which determines the level of net investment. Between the second and third years demand is still rising but the rate of increase has slowed down to 11.1 per cent and this causes the absolute level of investment to fall by 25 per cent. In year 4, a 5 per cent increase in demand leads to a 33.3 per cent decline in gross investment. Year 5 displays a similar pattern. In years 6 and 7 consumption remains at £21,500 and net investment falls to zero. Gross investment is £3,000, since capital consumed is still being replaced.

At the beginning of year 8 there is excess capacity of £500. Consumption falls to £20,000 and only £60,000 worth of capital is required to meet this demand. The capital in existence was £61,500 (capital stock in year 7 less depreciation). There is no need even to replace capital as it wears out in the eighth year. Total investment then fell to zero even though demand is considerably higher than it was in year 1.

The data illustrates how the rate of change in demand has a multiple effect on the change in net investment. Consequently, the swings in production levels are much greater for capital goods than they are for consumer goods.

(*c*) The accelerator theory contains a number of implicit assumptions. Firstly, it assumes that the capital–output ratio remains constant. In fact, technological advances are likely to reduce the capital–output ratio. When capital equipment is replaced, new machines may prove to be more efficient, so that increases in demand can be met without any increase in net investment.

A second assumption is that entrepreneurs consider any increase in demand to be permanent. If it is thought to be temporary, firms will respond by supplying from stock, allowing prices to rise or operating some form of rationing rather than buying new machines.

A third assumption is that the consumer goods industry is operating at full capacity; otherwise increased demand will be met by taking up slack. Conversely, the accelerator principle can only take effect if there is spare capacity in the capital goods industry.

Finally there is the assumption that any finance necessary for expansion is available for both capital and consumer goods industries at rates of interest which do not exceed expected profitability.

9

Economic Policy

QUESTION 1—TAXES ON EXPENDITURE

Shares of UK central government revenue raised by taxes on expenditure

Base of tax	Commodity	Percentage of central government revenue	
		1965	1976
Unit	Beer	3.3	1.8
	Wines and spirits	2.8	2.6
	Tobacco	9.9	4.2
	Oil	7.6	4.6
	Total of above	23.6	13.2
Ad valorem	Purchase tax	6.3	—
	Value added tax	—	9.4
	Car tax	—	0.5
	Total of above	6.3	9.9
	Total Customs and Excise★	33.6	25.4

★ Totals exceed detail because some minor items are omitted.

(Source: C. V. Brown and P. M. Jackson, *Public Sector Economics*, Martin Robertson, 1978)

(*a*) Explain the meaning of 'unit' and 'ad valorem' taxes.

(*b*) Comment on the above figures and on their implications for public policy.

[*January 1981, London*]

SUGGESTED ANSWER

(*a*) A 'unit' tax is a tax which is charged on a good in direct relation to the quantity of that good bought and sold. The tax is, therefore, the

101

same for each unit of measure of the good bought and sold whether that measure be one of length, area or volume.

Ad valorem taxes are related to the price of a commodity and are expressed as a percentage of that price. Thus, the higher the price of the commodity the greater is the amount of tax paid per physical unit of the good. The difference between the two types of indirect taxes can be shown by reference to the shift of the supply curve in appropriate diagrams.

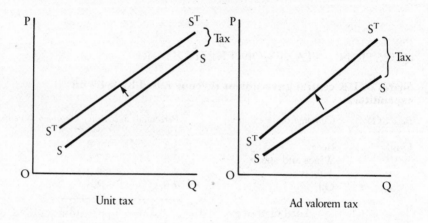

Unit tax   Ad valorem tax

(*b*) In 1965 the total percentage of government revenue raised by indirect taxes was 33.6 per cent, but this figure had fallen to 25.4 per cent by 1976. This change indicated a marked change in government policy which had begun to place greater emphasis on direct taxation. A second point is that within indirect taxation itself there was a greater proportional reduction in the revenue raised from unit taxes in the same period when compared with the fall in that raised from ad valorem taxes. Of the individual unit taxes mentioned in the question, tobacco declined most as a contributor to government revenue. It is a fact that the tax per unit of tobacco did not decrease in money terms between 1965 and 1976. It actually increased. The fall in contribution to revenue is, therefore, partly associated with a marked decrease in demand for the product—mainly as a response to the health hazards associated with smoking. In the short run, the government would look to other sources of revenue; but, in the long run, public policy in the provision of health services could be revised, as less medical care is required for patients suffering from the ill effects of smoking.

It is also a fact that, as in the case of alcohol, duties on the four commodities listed in the question were not increased annually in *real* terms. On the contrary, they fell in real terms. This point did not apply to VAT since this is based on selling prices which were increasing. For these reasons unit taxes contributed less to central government revenue in 1976 and ad valorem taxes increased their share of that revenue. Another significant change occurred in the case of the unit tax on oil. Here the main factor was a contraction of demand in response to the OPEC price rise for crude oil which took place at the end of 1973. Consumers tried to economise in their use of this much dearer form of power, so that tax yield fell in relative terms. The main issues for public policy concern the advisability of raising the level of tax on oil substitutes and the effects that this might have on inflation and employment, together with the need to encourage energy conservation in order to avoid inflationary cost increases. So far as alcoholic drinks are concerned, it is important to note that in this period the unit tax on beer was lower than that on wines and spirits. Pressure from the EEC to equalise these taxes raises a public policy issue for debate, since the figures indicate a fall in revenue from beer of greater importance than that for wines and spirits. Compliance with EEC policy could, therefore, further depress beer sales and increase wine sales. Were this to happen, there might be a fall in employment in the UK brewing industry, but a benefit to continental wine producers.

The main change in the ad valorem taxes was the phasing out of purchase tax (which was a selective tax), and its replacement by the very widely based value added tax. This was a move to harmonise UK fiscal policy with that of the EEC. Value added tax is even more regressive than purchase tax. Because a regressive tax calls for a much greater sacrifice by those on lower incomes than by those on higher incomes, it raises the question of public policy to decide which sections of the community should be exposed to the greatest tax burdens. One line of thought suggests that as taxes on expenditure can often be avoided simply by restricting one's purchases, the tax payer is allowed an element of choice which is lacking in the case of direct taxes such as income tax. On the other hand, it is argued that because direct taxes can be made progressive they share out the burden of taxation more equitably, and can be used to redistribute income in favour of the poorer population. A general shift away from indirect taxes is believed to slow down cost-push inflation, but if income tax were to rise significantly this could induce more inflation as higher money wages were demanded in order to protect the amount of take-home pay.

The second change in ad valorem taxation was the institution of the car tax between the dates given. As it is still a relatively new tax, it is not surprising that its contribution to central government was relatively small in 1976. However, it raises a public policy issue, because if the acquisition and/or operation of a car becomes more expensive, some people are likely to refrain from buying or using a car and will use public transport instead. A decision must then be made about the pricing and provision of appropriate public transport facilities. The broadest policy issue raised is whether there should be increases in direct taxes and/or increased public borrowing to compensate for the lower yield of indirect taxes. Here the choice will be influenced by such considerations as the consequences of the chosen course of action as it affects incentive to work, willingness/ability to save, and inflation.

QUESTION 2—URBAN SERVICES AND OPTIMAL CITY SIZE

'There has been much concern with the optimal size of towns and, in particular, with minimising the "per capita" costs of urban government services. The costs of these services have been observed to fall as a city expands, at a greater city size, start to increase again—a typical "U-shaped" cost curve. The minimum point of such a curve is the least cost, and hence optimal, city size.'

(Adapted from K. Button, *Urban Economics*, Macmillan Ltd)

(a) Explain why such cost curves might be U-shaped.
(b) What considerations, other than minimising per capita cost of government services, might be used to identify optimal city size?

[*June 1982, London*]

SUGGESTED ANSWER

(a) Costs are divided into fixed and variable groups. In the case of towns, fixed costs are those which must be met irrespective of the size of the population. The variable costs are those which change in response to changes in total population size. Average total cost curves are U-shaped because as population increases in a town the average fixed cost per capita decreases significantly at first. As an example of fixed costs, one can quote the capital outlays on sewage and refuse disposal, water purification and drainage of surface water. Variable costs per capita are also likely to fall at first, since many urban government services tend to be labour intensive, e.g. social workers. Thus, average total costs fall at first as economies of scale become possible. There is then likely to be a flat bottom to the U-shape of the average total cost curve which may extend over a range of total population figures. This is because the fall in average fixed costs has become very small indeed (for arithmetic reasons) while average variable costs may be contained by mechanisation of clerical work, e.g. the extended use of microprocessors and word processors.

Eventually, however, average variable costs do rise, particularly in the labour-intensive services where pay increases are very significant; or where less efficient labour has to be recruited in the long run. These are examples of dis-economies of scale to which all organisations become liable as the size of their operations increases.

(b) The optimum size of a city may not be that at which per capita cost is lowest. From a national income point of view the optimum size may be considered to be that at which output per capita is maximised, thus indicating that the population was being employed efficiently. Alternatively, one might consider the maximisation of income per household as being a valid criterion of optimum city size. Consideration can also be given to the number of employment opportunities offered by a city. This is of particular importance when unemployment is a national problem or when a city comes to rely on one main industry. In the latter case the enlargement of the city to accommodate more diverse kinds of jobs may be desirable. This may benefit not only those who live in the city but those who live in the surrounding area as well. The quality of life in the city is also an important consideration. For example, a city should be large enough to attract private enterprise to provide a range of shops, stores, leisure and entertainment facilities which will give the citizens the benefits of choice and competition so that their satisfactions may be maximised.

At the same time, social costs need to be minimised; so the city should not be of such a size as to generate excessive pollution or to reduce excessively the supply of rural land areas.

Finally, it is not sufficient to consider only the total population size of a city. It is also important to consider the mix of that population. There should be a balance of sex and age groups as well as a balance of occupational skills and educational opportunities. If any of these are lacking, the future well-being of the population could be at risk and there could also be a risk of increasing per capita costs.

QUESTION 3—UNEMPLOYMENT AND UNFILLED VACANCIES

Among other suggestions for dealing with the economic problems of the UK one proposal is the imposition of import controls as a means of rectifying an adverse balance of payments. Those who refute this suggestion do so in the belief that the balance of payments is not the problem which needs to be tackled since it has no direct link with slow economic growth and rising unemployment. Supporters of this view believe that even if the UK cut off all foreign trade there would still be the evils of inflation and costly energy supplies which would result in economic stagnation and loss of jobs.

Appraise the contradictory views expressed in this passage.

SUGGESTED ANSWER

The views expressed in this passage differ firstly in identifying the main problems of the UK economy in the late 1970s and early 1980s. In fact, the order of magnitude of these problems has changed radically as the years have passed. In the late 1970s the major problem was that of inflation whereas in the early 1980s greater emphasis could be placed on rising unemployment. As the perception of the problems has changed so, too, have the remedies put forward.

The view taken by advocates of import controls was probably based on the fact that if inflation is running at a high rate there must be a loss of competitiveness of UK exports in markets abroad where inflation is less, and prices of locally produced commodities therefore appear attractive to purchasers. Since the UK must import significant quantities of food and raw materials, any loss of export sales could, in the long run, lead to the need to cut imports to avoid adverse effects on the foreign exchange rate and reserves of foreign currencies. By the same reasoning, if prices rise excessively in the UK consumers will be tempted to substitute relatively cheaper imports for home produced commodities. This, in turn, would adversely affect foreign exchange rates and reserves of foreign currencies in the UK. It can be seen that if these effects on exports and imports continue then, through a derived demand effect, demand for labour in the UK will fall and unemployment will rise.

The remedy of import controls suggested would, if rigidly applied, prevent the substitution of home produced products by foreign ones. However, this would only tackle half the problem at most. It must be remembered that restrictions on exports *to* the UK may well provoke restrictions by foreigners on exports *from* the UK as they become faced with balance of payments problems.

The passage does not specify which form the import controls should take. The only really effective ones would be quotas, since demand for many UK imports is relatively price-inelastic and higher import duties would, therefore, make little reduction in the quantity of imports bought. In view of the foregoing, it is hardly realistic to say that unemployment has nothing to do with the balance of payments. After all, if high unemployment means reductions in purchasing power, the UK balance of payments might even be improved in the case of imported goods with high income elasticities of demand.

Slow growth (of domestic production) may, in times of affluence, be offset by the purchase of imports and so it is again an exaggeration to say that slow growth has nothing to do with the balance of payments.

So far as expensive energy is concerned, this was certainly a problem of the UK economy in the 1970s following the first OPEC price rise at the end of 1973 and before North Sea oil became available in large quantities. In fact this price rise started off cost-push inflation in the UK which triggered off high wage demands. As the rate of inflation increased, and wage costs mounted, employers were driven to economise in the use of both labour and energy. A multiplier-in-reverse effect occurred and the benefits of the accelerator effect on economic growth were lost. By the early 1980s the energy position had changed enormously with industry having become more fuel efficient and supplies of energy having increased from North Sea oil. Even OPEC prices of oil had fallen in both real and money terms by the end of 1982. To say that the UK economy would face problems of unemployment and slow growth if it had no foreign trade at all is a value judgement, since the statement is incapable of proof. It may, however, be that without trade the problems of unemployment and slow growth would be even worse. In recent years the UK balance of payments has more often than not been favourable, but this has been brought about mainly by the surplus on trade in oil. Since oil production is highly capital intensive and the non-oil sector (which is more labour intensive) has performed relatively badly, there has been a net loss of jobs. This loss of jobs may have been moderated because foreign trade exposes an economy to the stimulus of innovation from foreign ideas and products. This in the long run, is calculated to stimulate economic growth and the creation of new levels of employment.

QUESTION 4—COSTS, PRICES AND PROFITS

COSTS, PRICES AND PROFITS, 1968–78 (UNITED KINGDOM)

		Postal services	*Telecommunications*
% increase in real unit costs	1968–73	+21	−17
	1973–78	+13	−28
	1968–78	+37	−40
% increase in real staff costs per unit	1968–78	+48	−45
% increase in real wage costs per worker	1968–78	+37	+39
% increase in real prices	1968–73	+17	−19
	1973–78	+19	−14
	1968–78	+40	−30
Gross margin* (%)	1968	+3.7	+44.3
	1978	+6.5	+51.3

(*Gross margin = surplus as a percentage of revenue).

(Source: R. Pryke, *The Nationalised Industries*, Martin Robertson, 1981) (*a*) What do you understand by '% increase in real prices' in the above table?

(*b*) Discuss the view that, on the basis of these figures, the telecommunications industry is more efficient than the postal service.

[*January 1984, London*]

SUGGESTED ANSWER

(*a*) Prices measured in money terms are subject to fluctuation through the effects of inflation and deflation. During the years quoted in this question, money prices were increasing significantly because of inflation. For example, the purchasing power of the pound in 1970 had fallen by 1975 to about 59p. Putting this another way an article which had cost £1 in 1970 would have cost £1.70 in 1975, an increase of 70 per cent assuming that the articles were identical. The expression '% increase in real prices' means that price changes in money terms have been adjusted so as to remove the effects of inflation. In other words, it has been assumed that in general terms prices have remained constant, and so whatever changes have occurred reflect changes in real costs and profit margins rather than changes in the value of money.

(*b*) It is first necessary to define the word 'efficient'. Perhaps the most widely used definition in Economics is that efficient means production at the lowest possible average total cost. However, it is only in perfect markets that businesses achieve this whilst also earning a normal profit; and the two business activities given in this question enjoyed virtual monopolies in the years mentioned. It is therefore extremely unlikely that they were efficient in the sense of the word as already defined, although real unit costs fell by 40 per cent between 1968 and 1978 in the telecommunications industry. This was a more efficient performance than that of the postal services where the same costs rose by 37 per cent in the same period. A further look at costs reveals that real staff costs per unit fell in telecommunications whilst they rose significantly in postal services at a time when both industries were experiencing almost the same increases in real wage costs per worker. One can infer from this that there was a substitution of capital for labour in telecommunications but not in the postal services—which may therefore be accused of being less efficient. This substitution of capital for labour was made possible by the radical developments in technology which were taken up by the telecommunications industry during the 10-year period. These allowed the introduction of new services in data transmission and brought about an increase in demand, which almost certainly curtailed demand for postal services in general. New technology for the postal services was of less significance, partly because of the strong opposition from the Union of Post Office Workers to the introduction of new machines which would reduce significantly the numbers of workers required. As regards prices and profit margins, the telecommunications industry was able to reduce prices in real terms whilst prices for postal services were rising significantly in real terms. This may reflect not so much greater efficiency in telecommunications as the adoption of a marginal cost pricing policy in that industry. Another view of efficiency is the ability of a business to generate and increase profits in relation to the capital employed. No information is given about this latter figure, but the gross margin in telecommunications was always much higher than in the postal services. In the 10-year period, gross margins in the postal service showed much the greater proportionate increase, but on the whole the telecommunications industry may be considered the more efficient.

QUESTION 5—INCOMES POLICY

'The academic objection to incomes policy is based upon three propositions. The first is that independent wage-push is not the cause of inflation and so an incomes policy must eventually be frustrated because it does not tackle the root cause of the problem. This leads to the second point which is that, while an incomes policy can have no long-run effect, it will work in holding down wages in some areas, and so there will be distortions introduced in the process of allocating labour. The economy will thus be less efficient. Finally, and perhaps strongest of all, is the point that it has proved extremely difficult to demonstrate that incomes policies have had any significant effect at all in the UK in the last 25 years.'

(Source: K. A. Chrystal, *Controversies in British Macroeconomics*, Philip Allan, 1979)

(*a*) Discuss the meaning of 'independent wage-push' in the above passage.
(*b*) Critically evaluate the three objections stated and explain the nature of the 'root cause of the problem'.

[*January 1984, London*]

SUGGESTED ANSWER

(*a*) The term 'independent wage push' refers to an attempt made by organised labour to increase its share of national income—possibly at the expense of profits. In other words, the higher wages demanded do not represent a response by labour to an increase in final prices, but may be the response of labour to increased productivity. An increase in productivity can finance higher wage rates without pushing up unit wage costs, and this is the reason for asserting that independent wage push is not the cause of inflation. However, independent wage push (if successful) is likely to alter wage differentials and if this provokes attempts to restore these differentials (other things remaining the same) wage push is no longer independent and may well become inflationary as wage costs may amount, on average, to 70 per cent of total production costs.

(*b*) The first objection to an incomes policy can be criticised on the grounds that many producers work on a system of administered prices. That is to say they add a percentage mark-up to their costs. In this case *any* increase in total costs, e.g. as a result of an increase in the price of raw materials is going to result in a rise in the price of the products concerned. Rising prices then trigger wage demands and an inflationary spiral commences, particularly if there is excess demand for labour in the economy.

The second objection can be shown empirically to be valid. In the UK, the public sector is particularly important, as it is a substantial employer of labour. Consequently the government can, directly or indirectly, affect the level of wage settlements, and this it has done. For example, it has in some years deliberately held down wages of civil servants—direct intervention; and encouraged local authorities to hold down the wages and salaries of their employees—indirect intervention. However, these policies of wage restraint have not been uniformly applied, as is shown by the small wage increases given to teachers and the much larger increases allowed to the police. Other things being equal, this could be expected to distort the labour allocation process arising from wage levels freely determined. More people might be attracted to police work and fewer to teaching. Distortions between the public and private sectors are likely to be even more pronounced since an incomes policy is much more difficult to enforce in the private sector. Private employers have often circumvented regulations by redefining job specifications and/or titles. It has also been possible to avoid regulations by giving staff additional fringe benefits such as company cars, free meals and private medical insurance instead of cash payments.

A further point is that in holding down wage increases the government has sometimes insisted on a flat rate 'across the board' increase rather than a modest percentage increase.

Suppose that an increase of £4 per week is permitted for all instead of a 4 per cent increase. This means that a worker now earning £100 per week would then get £104, but one on £150 per week would only go up to £154. Thus, what was a 50 per cent differential is reduced to about 48 per cent. With each successive flat-rate increase, the differential percentage will fall further, and if the original differential was to reward acceptance of greater responsibility fewer people will seek such posts. Those already in posts of responsibility will resent the situation and may work less efficiently. In the long run, those adversely affected will try to 'catch up' when the incomes policy is relaxed and so initiate further inflation.

The final objection is substantiated by the experiences in the UK and Holland. In the 1970s they enjoyed short-term benefits in the control of inflation by an incomes policy, but organised labour won back most of its lost ground when such policies were relaxed. On the other hand, West Germany and Belgium made little use of incomes policies. In the end the progress of inflation in all four countries did not differ much. It may be that in the UK it was not so much the incomes policy itself which was at fault as the proliferation of trade unions which were able to bargain competitively for wage increases—often by 'leap-frogging' claims aimed at the preservation of differentials. It can also be argued that incomes policies in the UK from 1954 to 1979 were for the most part being employed at times of relatively full employment and so the threat of unemployment did not act as a deterrent to substantial wage claims.

The 'root cause of the problem' is an imbalance in the rate of increase in production of commodities and that of the money supply, if one accepts the monetarist view. Rising prices of essential imports (e.g. oil in 1973) and increases in indirect taxes (e.g. the rise in VAT to 15 per cent) have also been held responsible for more inflation, but the price rises attributable to these have, in general, been less than those attributable to higher wage costs. Apart from this 'cost-push' view of inflation it is possible that 'demand-pull' forces have been at work—and demand can only be made increasingly effective if consumers have more money at their disposal or the velocity of circulation increases.

QUESTION 6—PRIVATISATION

'It must be right to press ahead with the transfer of ownership from the state to private enterprise of as many public sector businesses as possible. . . . The introduction of competition must whenever possible be linked to a transfer of ownership to private citizens and away from the state. Real public ownership—that is ownership by people—must be and is our ultimate goal.' Mr Nicholas Ridley, Financial Secretary to the Treasury, 12 February 1982.   (Source: *Economic Progress Report*)

(a) State concisely what you understand by 'real public ownership'.

(*3 marks*)

(b) Explain the advantages likely to be gained from privatisation.

(*9 marks*)

(c) Outline the methods by which privatisation may be achieved.

(*8 marks*)

SUGGESTED ANSWER

(*a*) 'Real public ownership' as used in this question means ownership by individuals through widespread shareholding rather than ownership by large institutional investors (e.g. insurance companies, pension funds, etc.): or ownership by the state where important decisions are taken by those having no direct interest as owners.

(*b*) It is held by some people that privatisation will overcome a number of the deficiencies which have become apparent in public enterprises. If such enterprises are privatised, it is believed that more encouragement will be given to greater efficiency (particularly the reduction of costs); there will also be greater consumer choice (by allowing freer entry to an industry by competitors) and more innovation (both as regards methods of production and as regards new or improved products).

Whilst the level of costs may be regarded as a possible measure of efficiency, another is the rate of return on capital. In this respect, public enterprise in the UK is said to perform badly when compared with equivalent public enterprises abroad and with a number of private enterprises in the UK. An example of the former is the low level of labour productivity in the UK postal service compared with that of the same service in the USA. An example of the latter is the National Bus Company compared with various private enterprise coach operators. Privatisation must, therefore, have the better use of capital as an objective.

With regard to the objective of consumer choice, it is held that if more firms are allowed to enter an industry they may not only provide a variety of products, but also a variety of prices. This is because removing a monopoly/monopsony condition may weaken the powers of the trade union movement, with a consequent advantage in terms of lower labour costs. A further objective should be achieved by having more producers, namely the appearance of new and improved products as competition encourages innovation. Another objective of privatisation is to free management from political influence, so that management decisions may be taken more objectively. This seems desirable when one considers that managers of nationalised industries have often been obliged to take decisions for political reasons, and have been given quite different performance targets by different governments within relatively short periods of time.

Some Conservatives believe that a reduction in the level of public ownership will achieve the objective of making investment funds more readily available to competing private enterprises whilst at the same time reducing the PSBR, lowering the rate of increase in money supply, and hence fighting inflation. Finally, an objective of privatisation may be the improvement of the foreign trade position of the UK. Evidence which supports this view is provided by the failures of British Steel and British Leyland to hold their places in export markets, whereas private enterprises such as Marconi, Plessy and Racal have impressive export records.

(c) One method of transferring activities and assets from the public to the private sector is by the offer of shares to the general public as in the cases of Cable and Wireless, and Amersham International. This may not lead to 'real public ownership' since the shares may largely fall into the hands of a few large institutions. A further difficulty arises in fixing the issue price of such shares. If fixed too low it can lead to large windfall profits by those fortunate enough to get an allocation. If fixed too high the share issue may be partially left with underwriters who will incur unexpected losses. An alternative method is that of selling off an enterprise to a group of managers/employees as was the case with the National Freight Consortium. This is possible, however, only if the amount of capital required from each person is relatively small, since it is personal savings which provide this capital. A third alternative is that which has been tried in the NHS where in some hospitals catering activities and laundry services have been put out to tender. Here the activity is certainly privatised, though it is not always the case that ownership of the assets used is transferred to private ownership.

A fourth possibility is that of franchising. This could be done by regionalising a service such as the telephone service and offering the right to run the service in a region for a given period of time. The operator would become responsible for the provision of the service and the maintenance and expansion of fixed assets. For assuming these responsibilities the operator would keep part of the fees charged, paying a sum to a supervisory body which would exact certain standards of service and also review periodically the charges made for it. A precedent exists in the case of the franchises awarded by the IBA to various television companies.

10

Growth and Development

QUESTION 1—DISTRIBUTION OF WORLD INCOME

The following is taken from an address by the President of the World
Bank Group to the Board of Governors, Manila 1976.

	Percentage of world population	Annual income per capita 1965	1975
(a) Poorest nations	42	130	150
(b) Medium income developing countries	32	630	650
(c) Developed countries	26	4,200	5,500

Comment on these figures and on the economic problems which they
represent.   [June 1979, London]

SUGGESTED ANSWER

The figures illustrate the very substantial gap between the per capita
income enjoyed by people of the developed countries and the very low
levels found among the poorest nations. This gap widened in actual
relative terms between 1965 and 1975. In this period the poorest
nations showed an increase of just over 15 per cent; the developed
countries showed an increase of nearly 31 per cent. In relative terms
the medium income developing countries fared even worse with a
mere 3 per cent increase. There is, therefore, a continuing inequality in
the distribution of world income—the smallest percentage of world
population given in the statistics having by far the largest share of
income.

One of the reasons for this is that so many restrictions continue to
apply to world trade. Freer trade would enable the less developed
countries to earn more from exports to developed countries, but the
latter see cheap imports of, say, clothing and shoes, as importing
unemployment.

A main economic problem of all developing countries is that they
have low levels of education and health care coupled with poorly

developed infrastructures (they lack adequate transport networks, water and power distribution facilities and sanitation). The improvement of these conditions demands adequate resources of capital and skilled labour, but with such low levels of income people cannot be expected to save, and so local resources of capital are very limited. Where there are also deficiencies of important raw materials (e.g. oil in Brazil), it is quite impossible for a country, on its own, to raise income levels quickly.

Developed countries have attempted to make good some of these deficiencies of the poorer nations, particularly by providing loans of capital through their commercial banks and through international agencies such as the International Bank for Reconstruction and Development (the World Bank), and its sister organisation—the International Development Agency. Although the latter provides long-term loans at very low rates of interest, its resources nowhere nearly match the demand for funds. Lending by the commercial banks and the I.B.R.D. has caused increasing debt problems for the poorer and developing countries. Many have been unable even to meet the interest payments as they have become due, let alone repay the principal. All this places added strain on their balance of payments positions and in some cases has caused reductions in much needed imports of food and other necessities. It is also unfortunate for the poorer countries that some of the imports they need are the subject of marketing by cartels, as for example the oil supplies in the control of OPEC.

The actual size of the populations of the poorer and developing countries is yet another problem. If the growth of population in these areas could be reduced it would produce long term benefits. In the immediate future, however, benefits may be slow to appear since in most cases there is a high proportion of population under the age of 18 years and these young people constitute dependent, rather than economically productive, population. As these young people enter the working population they want, in many cases, to migrate from the rural to the urban areas (from primary production to secondary or tertiary production). When this occurs there may be adverse effects on local food production and the creation of social problems in towns. In this way increases in real income per capita are made even more difficult to achieve.

QUESTION 2—ECONOMIC GROWTH IN THE DEVELOPING WORLD

In the period 1965–73, output per head in developing countries with a per capita income in excess of $200 grew at 3 per cent per annum. The poorest developing countries with per capita incomes at or below $200 per head recorded a growth of output per head of just 1 per cent per annum. World Bank estimates predict rates for the decade of 3.5 per cent per annum for the 'richer' developed countries and a decline of 0.5 per cent per annum for poor developing countries. It has been calculated that the per capita income of the developing countries would have to grow on average at between 6 per cent (for Latin America) and 9.5 per cent (for East and South East Asia) per annum in the period 1965–2000 to prevent the absolute gap in per capita incomes widening between the EEC and the developing countries.

(Source: M. McQueen, *Britain, the EEC and the Developing World*, Heinemann Educational, 1977)

Comment on some of the alternative methods by which these problems might be alleviated.

[*January 1981, London*]

SUGGESTED ANSWER

Output per capita is a function of the total output achieved by a country in a given period and the size of its population in that period. Improved output per capita can, therefore, be achieved by increasing total output and/or preventing population increases.

It is apparent from statistics collected about the poor developing countries that they all have rates of population growth considerably above those of the 'richer' developed countries. These high rates of population growth result primarily from high birth rates and, to a lesser extent, from increasing expectations of life. One means of alleviating the problems mentioned in the question would be the adoption of programmes designed to encourage family planning and limitation of family size (as has been done in China). In the case of Latin America such a programme might encounter opposition on religious grounds but, if successful, would lead eventually to higher per capita incomes, due to a more optimum combination of production factors. Taking a shorter time span, it would seem better to tackle the problem of increasing total output. To do this three approaches are required—aid, trade, and education/training. Most poor developing countries suffer from a lack of capital (because low incomes leave little or no margin for saving), and often they also lack adequate food resources. It is argued that by making capital available to these countries they will be able to improve their infrastructures (especially communications and transport), and adopt more efficient means of production. Food aid may allow the population to work more effectively.

Aid programmes, however, are subject to criticisms. It is often held that bilateral aid is not always in the best interests of the developing country, since money thus provided may be subject to the condition that it be spent according to the wishes of the aid giver. This can lead to the purchase of items which are not of the price or type most beneficial to the recipient. On the other hand multilateral aid (e.g. from the World Bank, the I.M.F. or I.D.A.) has also been criticised on the grounds that the policies of the recipient government are subject to conditions laid down by a group of foreigners which involves some loss of sovereignty for the poor developing country. Another question is whether financial aid should take the form of gifts or loans. The former have the advantage of not producing subsequent difficulties of repayment, but gifts may (as mentioned earlier) be subject to burdensome restrictions on their use. Loans made by private enterprise banks are likely to burden recipients with future balance of payments problems when payments of interest and repayments of principle become due. This could also embarass the lending banks if they commit themselves to loans which are too large in relation to the banks' capitals. Loans made by other governments or by international agencies may also impose the same sort of burdens on future balances of payments.

Excessive lending to developing countries can raise interest rates in the lending countries with consequent difficulties there for economic growth and investment.

The poorer developing countries have goods of various kinds which they can export and so acquire funds which might otherwise have to be obtained as loans. Developed countries are, however, often unwilling to allow such trade to go on as it is said to undermine their own employment (e.g. in textiles). Attempts previously made in GATT and by the Lomé Convention to give better access to markets in developed countries need to be continued and improved upon. There may even be advantages in extending the sort of barter arrangements which have been made between the Soviet Union and India.

For most poor developing countries any significant increase in output per capita requires further conditions to be satisfied. One of these is stability of government and consistent government policies. These would attract private investment, especially from multinational companies whose bases are in more developed countries. The desirability of such investments is, however, questioned on the grounds that at least some future profits benefit shareholders outside the less developed country, and that these companies often take advantage of the low wages accepted by local people and usually bring in expatriate management. The economic power of multinational companies is sometimes greater than that of governments of less developed countries leading to some loss of sovereignty for these governments.

It is also desirable to improve the standards of education and training in the poorly developed countries so that the domestic labour force will have the skills and knowledge necessary to find employment as new business ventures are set up and obviate the need to employ foreigners.

QUESTION 3—GROWTH AND THE SMALL FIRM

'Substantial growth of the small firm sector is desirable as a means of reducing unemployment and improving the health of the economy in general. The economic environment is clearly the main influence on the growth of this sector. But in the present situation, that causality is reversed as the expansion of the small firms sector would be instrumental in the recovery of the economy.'

(Source: Martin Binks, 'Finance for the Expansion of the Small Firm', *Lloyds Bank Review*, October 1979.)

In the light of the above:

(*a*) How might the 'environment' affect the growth of the small firm?
(*b*) Discuss ways and means by which small firms could assist the recovery of the economy.

[January 1982, London]

SUGGESTED ANSWER

(*a*) The statistical definition of a small firm will vary according to the field of economic activity involved. In manufacturing industry, the Bolton Committee (1971) defined a small firm as one with less than 200 employees.

The 'environment' which affects the growth of the small firm relates to an economy with relatively high levels of demand, output and employment combined with stable prices. Under these conditions, existing small firms are more likely to expand and new ones to be created. A high level of economic activity will enable the small firm to benefit from additional external economies of scale and from increased demand for its goods and services. The latter may stem directly from consumers themselves or from larger firms requiring components and specialist equipment or services.

A significant increase in demand is often necessary before a small firm will be prepared to undertake any investment which represents a large proportionate increase in existing capital. This is a reflection of the accelerator process in which the level of net investment is a multiple greater than the change in output. Given the indivisibility of capital, any increase in demand must be considered substantial and permanent before the firm will respond.

Even if business confidence is buoyant, availability of finance may present a further obstacle to the growth of the small firm. Funds from family and friends or retained profits are limited. Nor can it appeal for finance to the general public or institutional investors since they usually prefer to fund large joint stock companies. Small firms typically rely on loan finance. Banks, however, are reluctant to supply them with loan capital since proportionately higher administration costs are involved and there is a greater risk of default on repayments. This particularly applies in times of recession. The Loan Guarantee Scheme is aimed at improving this aspect of the 'environment': the government underwrites 80 per cent of bank loans to small firms, although it makes a 3 per cent interest premium charge.

Expensive loan capital in short supply causes cash-flow problems for the small firm. A high rate of inflation will limit liquidity still further through the firm's functions as a trade creditor. Outstanding debts owed by customers may prevent the small firm from obtaining its own supplies of inputs because of inadequate cash reserves.

Large firms are in a stronger position to demand and obtain prompt payment for goods and services provided. Consequently, stable prices represent another element of the 'environment' conducive to the growth of small firms.

A stable political climate is also important, since small firms will be encouraged by consistent government policy on matters which are likely to affect production costs and/or demand.

(*b*) The data asserts that in the present situation causality is reversed and there are certainly a number of ways and means by which small firms could assist recovery of the economy. First, they are able to make a contribution to innovation. To take an example from the computer industry, Sinclair is a small firm which employed innovation as its major asset and others can be expected to play an important role in the development of new products. Second, small firms which are often under owner-management, display a greater degree of flexibility than larger firms in reacting to rapid changes in demand and technology. Small firms within the UK such as Godley & Creme have recently enjoyed considerable success in the production of promotion videos. The large film companies proved unable or unwilling to respond to rapidly changing techniques and fashions. Third, small firms may specialise in meeting the demand for personalised services or custom built goods. The restoration of classic cars and the manufacture of reproduction furniture are examples of consumer wants which large firms, reliant on economies of large-scale production, cannot cater for.

Specialist firms often sell a high proportion of their output in foreign markets, especially when single unit production is required. Any increase in exports would represent an additional stimulus to economic recovery. Fourth, small firms prevent complacency among large firms with which they may be in competition. As such they provide a spur to efficiency and innovation among existing market leaders determined to maintain their dominant position in the face of strong rivalry from small firms.

Any increase in investment, exports or consumption brought about by the activities of small firms, can be expected to have a multiplier effect on the economy as a whole. This, in turn, will create a wider range of employment opportunities in greater number. The small firm sector can, therefore, be instrumental in the recovery of the economy.

QUESTION 4—AGE DISTRIBUTION OF POPULATION— YEAR 2000

(*a*) Suggest reasons for the differences in the shapes of the age pyramids shown opposite giving projections for the year 2000.
(*b*) Assuming that these projections are realised discuss the economic problems likely to arise in these two regions.

Each part of the question carries 10 marks.

SUGGESTED ANSWER

(*a*) The age pyramid for the less developed regions is much more symmetrical than that for the more developed regions but it also tapers off more steeply in the upper age groups. The difference in symmetry is largely due to the fact that the population in the more developed regions has experienced the effects of major wars on certain age groups whereas such effects have been of minor significance in less developed regions. All of the major countries in the more developed regions were involved in the Second World War and, as a result, large numbers of males and some females died who would otherwise be likely to form part of the age groups over 75 years of age. In these more developed regions it is noteworthy that the age group 20–29 years is unusually small. This reflects the general fall in the birth rate of the 1970s. The small numbers in the age group 0–9 years were, of course, projections on the date when the statistics were published and

More Developed Regions

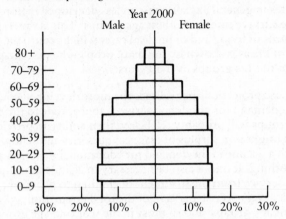

Less Developed Regions

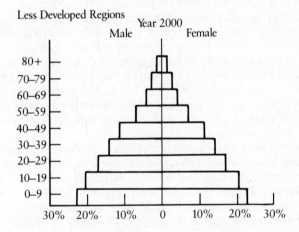

(Source: *Demographic Indicators of Countries* United Nations, 1982)

they assume a continued fall in the birth rate—partly because the putative parents group (20–29 years) is itself small. The age pyramid for the less developed regions reflects the traditionally higher birth rates of such places where, because of the lack of state provision for the elderly, families have tended to be large so that parents in their old age have enough children to support them. Another explanation of the higher birth rates is to be found in religious and social attitudes which do not favour ideas of contraception and family planning. The higher birth rates in these areas also represent a response to the higher mortality rates, especially in the first years of life. These higher mortality rates in general explain why, in less developed regions, fewer people survive into the highest age groups. This is the result of lower standards of living and of medical care, which reduce the expectation of life as is shown by the sharp drop in the percentages of population in the age groups over 50 years.

(*b*) Should these projections be realised, the more developed countries will find that demand for goods and services appropriate to the two lowest age groups will probably fall below their ability to provide them. There might be a surplus of places in nurseries and schools together with a decline in the demand for educational materials and children's clothing. It might also be necessary to change the emphasis in the health service from the treatment of children to provision for retired people. Well over 30 per cent of the total population will be in the dependent age groups, and so those in the working age groups will have to produce more or accept a lower standard of living in order to support a population with a heavy dependency ratio. More capital intensive forms of production may be required.

One of the largest age groups will be the 30–39 years group. This group will have reached a stage where many will have gained promotion in their jobs and still have twenty or more years to go to the retirement. Despite the smaller numbers in the 20–29 years group these people may find their promotions blocked by those above them in the age pyramid. As time goes by and the upper age groups expand, it may become increasingly difficult to provide them with adequate pensions.

The less developed regions will face different problems. Because of the very broad base of the age pyramid there will be a great demand for child-orientated products and services, especially health care and education. Nearly 40 per cent of the population will be 19 years of age or less, so a heavy burden will fall on the working age groups, especially if higher education is demanded. To some extent this burden may be reduced because of the small percentage of the population over the age of 60 years. However, should there be progress in the medical field the expectation of life will increase and the dependency ratio will become higher. Any fall in mortality rates will also produce difficulties both in housing and feeding the population. With such large numbers in the late teens and early twenties there will be a need for plenty of accommodation suitable for young couples and, ultimately, their families. Finally, many of these young people in the less developed regions will feel attracted by the higher standards of living of the more developed regions and the wisdom of restricting migration from the poorer to the richer regions will come into the reckoning.